PLANNING-
PROGRAMMING-
BUDGETING SYSTEM
(PPBS)

LIBRARY MANAGEMENT SERIES – No. 1
Sul H. Lee, Editor

Number one: Planning-Programming-Budgeting System; Implications for Library Management.

Number two: Legal Reference Collections for Non-Law Libraries: A Survey of Holdings in the Academic Community.

LIBRARY MANAGEMENT SERIES, NO. 1

PLANNING-PROGRAMMING-BUDGETING SYSTEM (PPBS)

Implications for Library Management

Edited
and with an Introduction by
SUL H. LEE
Acting Director of the Library
and
Associate Professor
Eastern Michigan University

Published for the
EASTERN MICHIGAN UNIVERSITY LIBRARY
Ypsilanti, Michigan
by
THE PIERIAN PRESS
Ann Arbor, Michigan
1973

Library of Congress Catalog Card No. 73-78314
ISBN 0-87650-040-8

THE PIERIAN PRESS
P.O. Box 1808
Ann Arbor, MI. 48106

CONTENTS

v

INTRODUCTION

Many conferences and meetings have been called to explore the ramifications of PPBS, and a number of questions have arisen in these sessions. For example: What is PPBS? What is it intended to do? How can it help? What are its strengths and weaknesses? Above all, what are its implications for the operation of a library?

In a concerted effort to search out meaningful answers to these questions, an Institute was convened at Eastern Michigan University. This publication is a compilation of the papers which were presented by the experienced practitioners of PPBS who participated in the Institute.

Richard Hall explains what PPBS is, and Donald Lelong details the implications for higher education. Harold Jenkins provides the illumination of his experience in using PPBS to improve library management, while Philip Jager describes the application of PPBS to higher education in Michigan. We learn from them that PPBS is not a panacea for all library problems, nor can it be implemented without careful planning. Its full potential will be achieved only through experience with the special problems encountered in applying PPBS to libraries.

The editor is grateful to Margaret Eide and Walter Fishman of Eastern Michigan University for their editorial assistance.

SUL H. LEE

Ann Arbor, Michigan
April 3, 1973

WELCOME TO EMU*

It is my pleasure to welcome you here to the Eastern Michigan University campus. The fact that you have been attracted by the announced subject, PPBS, is an indication that you are as concerned about doing your jobs as are those in other important offices of the the University who have the responsibilities of determining the future development of their programs. In fact, I suspect that some of you are anxious that there just might be a way of convincing the "powers that be" that only with a library that is strong and vibrant, can the school, college, or university be the strong institution of which they dream.

In simple terms, we will be talking about a system of relating planning to budgeting so that you will get your money's worth through analyzation of your program against what you should be doing in years to come in order to reach desired goals. If you have planned your budget on a year-to-year basis, as most of us have done, you have always had some idea of what you wanted to accomplish in five or ten years. PPBS is an effort to systematize the thinking processes by forcing you to be more definite in your long-range planning, to consider allied programs, and to see alternative courses of action for recommendation to the final decision maker — the legislature, the city council, the library board, or your University President.

The Planning, Programming and Budgeting System was used by Think Tank squads in the U. S. Department of Defense. During the 1960s they had the assignment of spending allotted dollars in the best way possible. They began their task with certain assumptions with which there will be little disagreement: (1) public funds are limited, (2) the controllable portion of the budget is small in any given year, (3) innovations are difficult to implement, and likewise, some existing programs may have outlived their time, (4) there is a need for a link between long-range plans and budgets, and (5) there is a need for constant monitoring and evaluation of all on-going programs.[1]

Here at Eastern we are concerned about any system which will help us to put over our program. Though this institution has been

    * a welcoming address by A. P. Marshall, Director Eastern Michigan University, Ypsilanti, Michigan at the Institute on Library Management — PPBS on April 21, 1971.

1 Bromberg, Erik, "Simplified PPBS for the Librarian". Manuscript.

in existence since 1849, it is only recently that we have gone "big league". Like librarians at many such universities, we are not worshippers of money **per se,** but we know that it takes money to bring our library collection up to a respectable level. We would like to achieve this growth at once but the facts of financial capability are ever with us. Sometimes we find ourselves in the position of the young college freshman who sent a letter to his dad: "Dear dad, I am broke and have no friends. What shall I do?" His father wrote back: "Make friends at once."

In one sense we are very fortunate. We have an administration which is very responsive to library needs. This resulted in a new library building in 1967, a dedicated staff which is one of the most responsive to student needs that you will find anywhere, and an increasing share of the total university budget which, even in periods of recession, has provided continual growth and development.

We may not have the rich resources of those university libraries which have enjoyed a long and distinguished career in the big leagues but we, perhaps (like Avis), try harder. During this year we have developed some long-range plans as much for our guidance as for a basis for PPBS. At the moment, our books are bulging on the shelves. In asking for additional shelf storage, we even offered some alternatives. There are two basic ones: We can stop buying books, which will bring down the wrath of both students and faculty alike for not supplying them with needed resources; or, we can remove some of our books from the shelves and place them in boxes in the basement, which will also prevent our students and faculty from getting at the resources they need. It is well recognized among librarians that students seldom want books which are on the shelves. It is always those that are out which are in demand.

If you have the opportunity to do so, we invite you to see some of our campus. At least we hope you will visit our rather modern library. And if, while here, there is help needed which we can provide, do not hesitate to make your wishes known. We have no pull at all with the Police Department, neither campus nor city. But, of course, librarians are not likely to be unable to avoid trouble, nor to talk themselves out of it should it come.

Let us suffice these brief remarks with the well-known and well-used words: Welcome to our campus and to our city. Enjoy yourselves, and come again when you can stay longer.
4/21/72

PROGRAM BUDGETING — WHY?

Richard W. Hall, Comptroller

Eastern Michigan University

The subject of this institute as you know, is "PPBS, Implications and Applications". And as you also know, if you opened the cover of your folder, "PPBS" is an acronym for Planning-Programming-Budgeting System. As I am sure Mr. Sturtz will inform you, the State of Michigan's version of this operation is "PBES" or the Program Budget Evaluation System.

My purpose this morning is not to explain subtle differences in semantics or introduce a new vernacular into your vocabulary, but rather to convince you that program budgeting is not really new. And to show that it is a natural step in the evolution of management techniques designed to assist in accomplishing the reclassification of decision making from an art to a science.

In the early days, "budgets" resulted from and reflected the answer to only one basic question, "How much?" A budget simply showed how much it was estimated a given plan or project would cost. The problem with this approach was that if the actual cost exceeded "budget" there was no basis for explaining why and the one preparing the budget usually took the blame for a bad estimate. As a professional in the budget field I can assure you that this was not an acceptable state of affairs and it was not long before the basic concept of "performance measurement" came into the picture. However, performance measurement required that one question be answered in addition to "how much?" and that was "what for?"

As it turned out, this combination of questions was the key which released the budget analyst from his accountant's corner and green eye shade and admitted him to the ranks of operating management. It was found that "how much" and "what for" were so interdependent that the one preparing a budget was required to question the basic plans of management as to their intent and objectives. While this was not always a popular position to be in, especially when dealing with managers who were used to "flying by the seat of their pants", it is a situation which has prevailed. As business and government have become larger and more complex, the number of managers who can survive exclusively on the basis of institute judgement has decreased, and the need for a scientific

3

approach to management planning and decision making has become well established.

The answers to the question "what for" were phrased in terms of the objects for which the total budget would be spent, such as salaries and wages, supplies, services such as telephone and utilities, and equipment. Since these items of expense were usually summarized with the item and amount to be spent shown on the same line, they came to be known as "line-item" budgets.

The early "line-item" budgets provided a basis for evaluating, after-the-fact, the degree to which the budget estimates were accomplished and provided a basis for determining whether the variance was due to an invalid budget, or inefficiency on the part of those doing the job. For the budget expert, this was a very satisfactory situation and for a time his efforts were directed toward expanding the line-item budget concept by constantly increasing the degree of detail in the budget and refining analytical techniques for handling non-monetary data use in the development of the line-item, or "object" budget. His purpose was the precise analysis of any variance from budgeted levels and the pinpointing of responsibility for that variance, whether favorable or unfavorable. This approach provided management with a wealth of information which they had not had previously and gave them an ability to control their operations and a basis for making operating decisions unsurpassed in history.

Unfortunately, in my opinion, the problems we face today in the area of budgeting are the direct result of higher education. It is the result of all those misguided professors who kept trying to instill in their students a sense of inquiry. You see, some time ago, when a sincere budget director was earnestly seeking answers to the questions of "how much?" and "what for?" a smart aleck college graduate came along and asked "why?"

"Why?" The first question which crossed the budget director's mind probably was "what does that have to do with budgeting?" After all, budgets are based on quantifiable data. If you can't express it in numbers, you can't measure it, and if you can't measure it, how can it be part of a budget.

In defense of the budget director, let me say that the ability to be measured is a prime requisite for including any element in a budget process. However, the fallacy in his thinking lay in his presumption that the answer to the question "why?" could not be quantified.

Let's assume that this budget director was a particularly intelligent fellow, say an ex-professor who had to go to work for a living, and that he took his young associate up to the president of the company, a manufacturing and sales organization, to ask him the question of "why?" Let's further assume that the president was a nice guy with a father-complex who wanted to try and help straighten out this young man. With this in mind, the president patiently explained that all of the operations and programs of the company had only one objective, to make a profit.

This should have solved all the problems since net profit was the bottom line on the budget and therefore the answer to why was not only clear, but quantified. Unfortunately, the young man's inquiring mind had been overdeveloped and he asked the president one more question "why do you spend money on a product guarantee program?"

Again, patiently, the president responded by explaining how a product guarantee program improves the product image in the marketplace and improves customer satisfaction thus having both a favorable current and long run effect on sales volume and hence on profits. Did this satisfy our young trouble-maker? No. Unfortunately, he knew enough accounting to know that the product guarantee program showed up as an expense in the budget and therefore resulted in an apparent reduction in net profit. Now, we know that what the president said was true, don't we? We know it intuitively, don't we? And yet, if you were the president of that company, how would you answer the young man's next questions which were:

> "What would happen to net profit if the product guarantee program were dropped?"

> "What would happen to net profit if the scope, or some other feature of the product guarantee program were changed?"

The budget director probably responded that the existence and scope of the guarantee program was based on experience and competition. Unfortunately, "competition" or "what others are doing" is frequently the explanation for an action or program used by someone who doesn't really know the answer to "why?"

Going back to the young man's last two questions, I want to point out that, despite their wording, they really are only one question, and that is "Why does this company have the product guarantee program that it has?" Also, I want to point out that, while the answer to this one question, the answer which the president gave, defies quantification, the alternatives expressed by the two separate questions can readily be quantified through the use of modern market research techniques.

Now I don't know what happened to the young man. If the little scene I described took place twenty five years ago, there is a good chance he was fired. There was a period when top management, having come up the hard way through the ranks, felt insecure and challenged by new ideas and new techniques. However, change the time to five years ago, and the chances are he was made head of the Program Budgeting Department. I assume that most, if not all, of you are directly involved in library management or administration, and as such have already learned that the successful manager in today's complex society is not the one with all the right answers, but rather the one who asks all the right questions.

Program budgeting has been with us, at least in major industries, for two decades or more. It has spread to more and smaller companies because those companies soon found themselves at a competitive disadvantage if they were unable to answer the kind of questions generated by a program budgeting system. Of course, a major reason for the spread of the program budget concept through the profit oriented segment of the economy is that with profits as a motivating factor the "why?" type questions can most readily be answered in terms which permit quantification and hence can be adapted to budget computations.

A program budget system can be described as performing three basic functions for management in the decision making process. First it provides a catalyst or stimulant to the planning process. To function properly a program budget system requires a substantial quantity of refined input data. This forces the management team to overcome a tendency to plan superficially and avoid decisions which may be difficult, but not impossible, to quantify. It forces management to plan on a comprehensive basis, including all phases of the operation, because programs usually transcend jurisdictional and organizational lines. In short, program budgeting requires the involvement of the total management organization in the planning process.

Second, program budgeting provides the common denominator by means of which the diverse elements involved in a program can be brought together and related in a meaningful manner. Note that does not mean that all elements have to be reduced to monetary expression, although this will be true for most of the elements. What it does mean is that program budgeting requires the development of means to measure all aspects of a program so that meaningful relationships can be developed between the component inputs, outputs and objectives.

And finally, and perhaps this is really just an extension of the second function, it provides a guide for management to use in making the final decision whether or not to implement or continue the program as structured. It allows management to compare the resources required by the program with the degree to which the objectives of the program are expected to be accomplished, and make a value judgment as to the wisdom of using those resources in that way.

Allow me to draw on my experience as a financial analyst with the Ford Motor Company to attempt to illustrate how program budgeting can actually work in an industrial setting. Keep in mind that, in this situation, the question of "why?" was readily answered and quantified in terms of net profit and return on investment.

Along about 1959, a relative newcomer on the automotive scene, American Motors Corporation, was chiding the "Big Three" about their "Gas Guzzling Monsters" and successfully selling a line of low powered economical cars called Ramblers. During this same period the little German car affectionately known as the "Bug" or "VW" was demonstrating a trend of increasing sales which was continued largely unabated.

These conditions did not escape the attention of Robert S. McNamara who was then General Manager of the Ford Division and a strong proponent of the concept of program budgeting as a management tool. It was largely through his influence that the Ford Division undertook a program designed to produce a low cost economical car which would be direct competition for the Volkswagen. And it was at his insistence and under his direction that a program budget was established and updated on a monthly basis to provide the essential data required in making decisions as the program envolved. Again I will remind you that the answer to "Why was this project undertaken" was to produce profit, and the amount of profit required was defined. While this may seem to be a simple point, I hope to show how the fact that this objective was clearly stated and quantified played a key role in the decision process.

First, it must be recognized that, at that time, the Ford Division was a combination assembly and sales operation. It did not have the capability to design, engineer, and produce a complete vehicle. Consequently it was immediately clear that the small car program required cooperation and coordination among many operational areas. Central Styling was one of the first groups involved with both Ford Motor Company and Ford Division engineering staffs joining the program almost simultaneously.

Even at this early stage, the program budget required decisions to be made relative to the proposed market price of the vehicle, estimated sales volume, and related cost and profit estimates. In essence, the combination of sales price and volume set the limits within which the designers and engineers were required to work. Every time a styling change was introduced, the effect on the cost of sheetmetal, tooling, and assembly had to be calculated to see if the styling change could be contained within the budget parameters. Engineering changes in the chassis and drivetrain had to undergo similar analysis. And of course, what made it fun was when both styling and engineering changes were proposed simultaneously, and in some cases were interrelated and had to be evaulated on a combined basis.

As the plans evolved beyond a certain point, other units of the company were brought into the program picture such as the Engine and Foundry Division, Metal Stamping Division, Standard Transmission Division, etc. As these other organizations were familiarized with the program, cost estimates of components which they would produce, which had been developed by analysts and engineers, were reviewed by people close to the actual production process and necessary revision in the budget estimates made accordingly. This particular program was further complicated by decisions to fabricate certain major components in Europe and ship them to the United States by sea. This required review of potential import and export duties, foreign exchange rates, shipping costs, etc. All of the data had to be fed into the program budget to see if the primary objective could still be met. Obviously, if that objective had not been clearly stated in measurable terms, the ability of the program to meet that objective would also have been unmeasurable.

I don't want to give the impression that a program must have only one well defined objective. In many cases a program may have a combination of objectives which can or must be met. However, one is usually considered primary while others may be considered mandatory parameters rather than objectives. In the case of the small car program, the other controlling objectives were safety, durability and economy. Of these, safety would have to be considered a mandatory parameter while the other two could vary, within limits, depending on the effect on profits.

By 1961 the small car had been dubbed the "Cardinal" and was scheduled for introduction in the domestic market as a 1963 model in the Fall of 1962. During the development of the Cardinal, Market Research had been busy in continually analysing the activity in the segment of the market in which the Cardinal was intended to compete. Price and sales fluctuations of competing products had been carefully noted and the long range prospects for that market segment predicted.

Less than eighteen months prior to the proposed introduction date, a careful review of the program was ordered because the estimates in the program budget showed a disturbing picture. Costs had risen beyond expectations due to inflation as well as to required engineering changes. To meet the profit objective (which was clearly defined), it would be necessary to market the vehicle at a price that was higher in relation to competition than had been planned. However, market research indicated that at the higher market price, planned volume would not be obtained and therefore the profit objective would still not be met. In fact, because of the high fixed costs involved, a net loss could result.

To make a long story short, because the primary objective of the program could not be met, based on data drawn from the program budget, the decision was made to cancel the program and write off approximately $50,000,000 in sunk costs. In other words, it was decided that it was wiser to lose the resources already committed to the project by cancelling it than to commit the additional resources necessary to complete it.

As I have stressed repeatedly, the ability to quantify and

measure all elements of a program is critical to the development of a program budgeting system. And this undoubtedly explains why the spread of the program budget concept to the non-profit segment of the economy, especially government, and specifically higher education has been slow and difficult. The problem, of course, lies in the answer to the question "Why?" which can be asked about any governmental or educational program. It is sometimes difficult to get any answer to this question, let alone an answer which can be reduced to measurable terms. **Why** is the state of Michigan embarking on the PBES program? I wonder if Mr. Sturtz can give me a measurable answer to that question. **Why** do we have a music program here at Eastern? I know why, but how can I quantify it. **Why** do you need more books in your library? Give me an answer to that one I can measure. Notice I didn't ask how many books you may need, but why?

Gentlemen, I am sure that the subsequent speakers today will explain in detail exactly how you should go about answering all of the "why" questions you can expect to be asked as program budgeting evolves at your institution. Included in their answers may be the suggestion that the questions be rephrased, or that measuring techniques need to be refined, or even that new methods of measurement need to be developed to cope with the intangible. But one answer I don't expect to hear is that measurement is impossible and therefore program budgeting should be abandoned. In the State of Michigan, the "why" questions being directed to the government, and through the government to higher education, are coming, basically, from the taxpayers. To tell the taxpayers their questions can't be answered is tantamount to handing in your resignation. And I think rightly so.

The mechanics of program budgeting are relatively simple in concept and relatively easy to describe in general terms. It is the implementation which causes a few problems. The first step is the redefinition of the total operating picture of the budget unit in terms of programs. Most operations are organized along lines of authority and responsibility with cost and revenue centers constituting the control substructure. Notice, I said the first step is redefining, **not** reorganizing. Program budgeting will normally have little or no effect on the existing organization structure of the budget unit. Notice also I said redefinition of the **total** operating picture. Up to this point the discussion has dealt with individual program examples which could in fact be considered simply as special analyses. One of the major benefits to be derived from a comprehensive program budget system is the introduction of the "zero base" concept in management planning. Let me explain.

A more or less standard approach to budget preparation for years has been to ask four basic questions.

1. How much does the present level activity cost?
2. What change will result from external economic factors?

3. What change in level of present activities is planned?
4. What new plans or activities are proposed?

This approach has a great deal of merit, but it includes one major fallacy.It presupposes that the present level of activity and the programs included therein have been justified and validated in prior years and are therefore still acceptable. In other words, it uses the present level of activity as a base and focuses analysis and planning on possible departures from that level of activity.

On the other hand, a program budget system requires that each program, present and proposed, be reviewed each time it is funded to insure that allocation, or continued allocation, of resources to that program is justified. In short, it starts with zero activity as a base and directs analysis and planning efforts toward the total program.

The only real problems inherent in this first step of redefining operations lies in determining what actually constitute programs. Oddly enough, one of the best ways to resolve these problems is to, in a sense, work backwards and define the objectives of the business or institution. Once the objectives are clearly defined, it is necessary only to group the resources and activities in terms of the objectives they assist in reaching and you have programs delineated. Of course, this presumes that management has solved the basic problem of clearly defining, in measurable terms, the objectives of the operation.

At this point let me comment that one of the technical and yet critical factors which management must consider in dealing with the question of objectives is the minimum level of aggregation at which those objectives should be expressed. At one extreme, the entire operation of a complex organization could be said to be directed toward one objective, let's say profit. This would constitute a simple solution to management's problem in that all elements and resources would be components of a single program and program budgeting would be meaningless. The other extreme of course would be to state objectives with such precision and at such a low level that the multitude of programs resulting would require a program budget department of such magnitude that the cost would put the operation out of business. This is just another illustration of the fact that a program budget system does not replace management judgement but it does give it a lot of exercise.

Once the program outlines are established, the second step in a program budget system is the accumulation of necessary data, both accounting and non-accounting, in the program format. If the amount of data involved is substantial, relatively simple computer systems can be used to perform the operation of re-sorting data from the normal accounting format to a program format. Normally no significant change in the accounting system would be contemplated since the informational needs served by the present system will continue. If a change is made, it would not be toward a program alignment, but rather toward a data base concept which would provide a pool of data which could be tapped in whatever manner was desired.

The final step in a program budget system is the frequent monitoring of the operations with particular emphasis on the degree to which the objectives are being accomplished. Without this final step the entire system will collapse of its own weight. It is this final step which provides management with the information essential in making on-going program decisions, validates original estimates included in the budget, and insures understanding of and compliance with management plans throughout the organization.

Going back to the title of this Institute, let me suggest that the term PPBS, while it springs from an honest desire to reflect all of the elements in the system — planning, programming, and budgeting — is cumbersome and imprecise in that the three elements are interrelated and interdependent and not separable. As you are aware, I have used the term program budgeting to include all three activities. I think the State's acronym PBES is more descriptive of the purpose of the system, which is program budget evaluation. However, even here I suggest that the term "budget" is superfluous and that the most precise statement of the objective of program budgeting can be expressed in three letters "PES" for program evaluation system. After all, the ultimate objective of any of these systems, whether used in business, government, or higher education, is to insure, if possible, that the limited resources available are employed in the best and most desirable programs.

In closing, let me mention just a few things that a program budget will not do. It will not make decisions for you. It will not function more effectively than the quality of the input data will allow. And in its present form, it will not provide the necessary data required for daily operations control and the making of short-run operating decisions.

This last point is important because it means that operating budgets as you and I know them will continue to be required and will continue to provide management with a tool vital to the smooth functioning of the department or institution.

PLANNING, PROGRAMMING, BUDGETING SYSTEMS IN HIGHER EDUCATION[1]

Donald C. Delong

Director, Office of Institutional Research
The University of Michigan

My assignment today is to explore with you some of the virtues and vices of planning, programming, budgeting systems as those systems apply to higher education. Perhaps the best way to attack the subject is first to say a few words about the need for better planning and budgeting in our colleges and universities; second to describe briefly the primary focus of the PPBS approach. Third, you ought to have some idea, if you don't already, of the rather staggering information requirements which generally accompany program budgeting systems, and finally I would like to suggest some of the major conceptual issues posed by planning, programming, budgeting methods.

THE NEED FOR BETTER PLANNING AND BUDGETING

First then, a few words about the need. We in higher education are being pressed as never before to tell just what we are doing, why we are doing it, and how much it costs. Let me use my own university as nothing more than an illustrative example. During the last twenty years Michigan state government expenditures on higher education have climbed much more rapidly than government expenditures in other areas. As Figure 1 shows, operating appropriations to higher education have increased over 900% since 1950, while total government expenditures have increased at only about half that rate. Under these circumstances we certainly shouldn't be surprised to have legislators and citizens asking how long this rate of growth can continue. Nor should we be surprised when they ask about the economic and social benefits which are produced with all of these dollars.

A second good reason for a more careful look at our resource use is that our university, like many others, represents complex enterprise on a large scale. Most colleges and universities spend milions every year, and the larger ones hundreds of millions annually. Their presidents and executive officers cannot possibly maintain an intimate understanding of all the facets of institu-

---

1 Portions of this paper are reprinted from the "Proceedings of Symposium on Accountability in Higher Education" held at Florida State Universersity, Tallahassee, Florida, October 21, 1971.

FIGURE 1

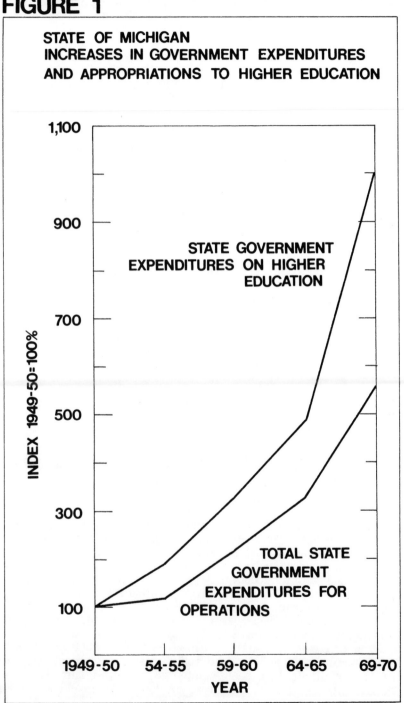

STATE OF MICHIGAN
INCREASES IN GOVERNMENT EXPENDITURES
AND APPROPRIATIONS TO HIGHER EDUCATION

STATE GOVERNMENT
EXPENDITURES ON HIGHER
EDUCATION

TOTAL STATE
GOVERNMENT
EXPENDITURES FOR
OPERATIONS

INDEX 1949-50=100%

1,100

900

700

500

300

100

1949-50   54-55   59-60   64-65   69-70

YEAR

tional operations. As resource allocation decisions move from the academic department, to the college, to the central administration of the university, to state government, those decisions are necessarily and inevitably based less and less on an intimate and thorough understanding of the operation being budgeted and more and more on some objectivised, quantitative information. In the absence of competent analysis of resource utilization, decision makers at the central university and at the state levels are left largely with random impressions, preconceived notions, and quite possibly with political pressures in the parochial sense of that term.

Finally, better planning and budgeting should also help us meet the leveling and even declining enrollments in the years ahead. Note that according to the U. S. Office of Education Projection, shown in Figure 2, total enrollment in higher education will top out about 1980 and then bottom-out about 1988. Though this projection includes a constantly increasing percentage of high school graduates going on to college, that increase is not sufficient to overcome a dip in the absolute numbers of college-age youths through the 80's. Those of you who have managed library budgets through periods of enrollment growth know that it is possible to correct a multitude of sinful misallocations through the blessings of incremental adjustments. However, if we are going to maintain innovative and responsive programs during the coming decade, we shall have to learn the art and science of generating new monies internally. That in turn will require much better evaluative information than we now have available about the utilization of resources by college or university programs.

PRIMARY FOCUS OF PROGRAM BUDGETING

This brings me to the major focus or the principal benefits claimed for the PPBS approach. I don't know how familiar most of you are with the program budget approach, but the advantages claimed for it are several. One is that it represents a systematic attack on the allocation and utilization of all the resources available to an organization. Instead of hurriedly scratching out one's budget needs for the coming year a day or two before the deadline for submitting the budget request, PPBS requires that you take a long range look at your operation and articulate just what you hope to accomplish over a three to five year period. Then it is necessary to lay out specific programs of action which will enable you to accomplish your stated objectives. Ideally the program analyst lays out several alternative means of accomplishing a program objective, if several alternatives are available. Next all of the resources required, such as manpower, supplies and equipment, etc. have to be spelled out for each program. In fact, a program is usually defined as that collection of activities and resources needed to accomplish a specific objective. Once all of this analysis has been completed, the program resource requirements are costed in terms of dollars to produce a program

FIGURE 2

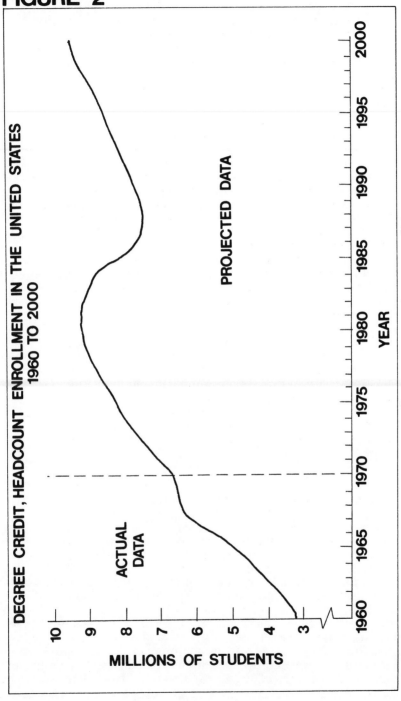

DEGREE CREDIT, HEADCOUNT ENROLLMENT IN THE UNITED STATES
1960 TO 2000

ACTUAL
DATA

PROJECTED DATA

MILLIONS OF STUDENTS

YEAR

budget. The somewhat unusual value of the program budget over the conventional budget lies in its ability to pull together all of the activities and resources dedicated to the accomplishment of a specific purpose. For example, if one of the objectives of an institution is to graduate competent electrical engineers, then all of the resources devoted to electrical engineering students and all of the activities undertaken in behalf of their education, whether within the department of electrical engineering or elsewhere in the university, would represent a single instructional program.

Actually, the program approach to both budgeting and resource analysis really adds a third dimension to two other dimensions which have long been used to describe university operations. As the solid block in Figure 3 illustrates, the academic operations of a university are conventionally described in terms of the resources used, such as staff, facilities, and equipment, and also according to the organizational units making up the institution — that is, resources allocated to the College of Architecture and Design, Business Administration, etc. We have long combined the object classification (that is the type of resource) and the organizational unit to describe university operations. In a Program Budgeting and Costing system, however, the program dimension is added to the other two, not substituted for them as some critics of PPBS seem to think. This means that program budgeting takes a lot more time and energy than conventional budgeting. Notice that the programs of instruction, research, and public service cut across all types of resources and all organizational units. Program budgeting and program costing attach great importance to the fact that the program dimension is the one which is most logically associated with outputs and results of institutional operations. It is therefore the program dimension which permits an institution to account for its resources in terms which are not only most meaningful to its own substantive planning but also meaningful to the public and to other sources of funding.

In fact, there is also a fourth dimension to operating in any good PPB system. Not only must we look at resource utilization by type of resource, by organizational unit, and by institutional purpose, but we must look it in terms of sources of funding. In Figure 4 we have merely picked off the top layer of the previous chart — the layer which refers only to one organizational unit, the College of Architecture and Design. For that unit, as well as for all the others, we need to examine which fund sources support which programms. If we can do that, then we can assure the Federal Agency, for example, that its funds did indeed support the research project which it intended, or the state that its funds did indeed support the programs for which we requested the money. So a good system of program budgeting really needs to be accompanied by a good system of program costing. The latter will permit us to account for resource expenditures by program and purpose, and also confirm to fund sources that their monies were

FIGURE 3

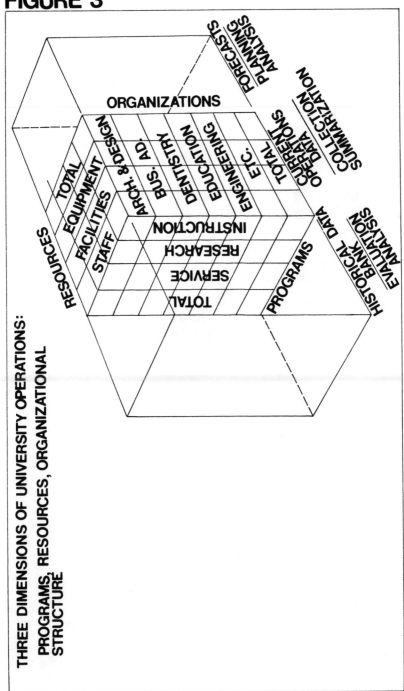

THREE DIMENSIONS OF UNIVERSITY OPERATIONS:
PROGRAMS, RESOURCES, ORGANIZATIONAL STRUCTURE

FIGURE 4

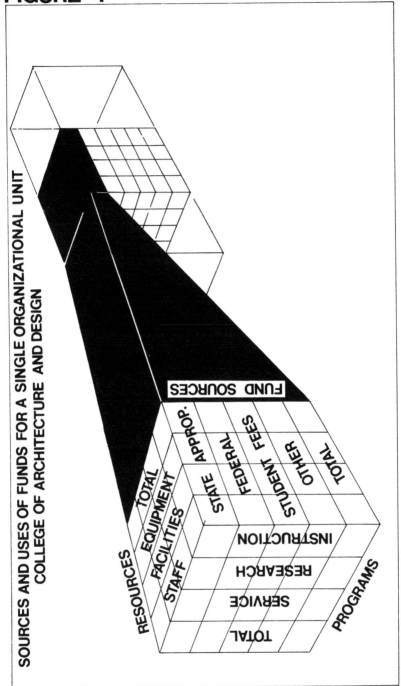

SOURCES AND USES OF FUNDS FOR A SINGLE ORGANIZATIONAL UNIT
COLLEGE OF ARCHITECTURE AND DESIGN

FUND SOURCES

RESOURCES
TOTAL
EQUIPMENT
FACILITIES
STAFF

STATE APPROP.
FEDERAL
STUDENT FEES
OTHER
TOTAL

INSTRUCTION
RESEARCH
SERVICE
TOTAL

PROGRAMS

used for the purposes intended. This is certainly no small order, given the conventional budgeting and accounting information currently existing at most institutions, including my own. The number of universities and state governments which are attempting to launch program budgeting systems without the benefit of program cost information is simply astounding! It will be even more amazing if they get anything useful out of their efforts; I just do not see how that is possible.

INFORMATION NEEDS FOR PPBS

This brings us to the subject of program information requirements. Virtually all of the managerial data we have collected in the past has been on an organizational unit basis. As Figure 5 illustrates, we know a lot about the chemistry department and how it spends its money. We also have a great deal of information concerning students taught by the department and some data on research and public service activities of the department. Unfortunately these data have never been organized on a program basis. What we need is information about the resources utilized in educating chemistry majors, as illustrated in Figure 6. This has not been compiled regularly. Obviously the student majoring in Chemistry might take courses in mathematics, English, history, and any number of other departments. He undoubtedly utilizes the services not only of the library but also the student health center, perhaps museums, and any number of other facilities. The task of building this sort of program information is not conceptually difficult, but it is extremely complex and time consuming, and it poses a number of horrendous practical problems.

At the moment, six public colleges and universities in Michigan are just completing a Pilot Project designed to find out how difficult it would be to collect good program cost information that would give us a good basis for planning and program budgeting. We have each tried to examine the programs in only three academic departments and to collect data telling us how much it really costs to run each program of each of these departments. The cost of library services has been an extremely difficult problem because most of us have no information about the extent to which undergraduate chemistry majors, for example, utilize the services of the library, compared to graduate students in foreign languages. Yet this is the sort of data we need to do a refined job of constructing budgets on a program basis. In fact, in our university, and I am sure in most others, competent planning, programming, and budgeting implies an almost entirely new and additional information system.

Since one of the best ways to describe the defacto purposes of an institution is to describe what its faculty is actually doing, and since faculty salaries represent the largest single item in most academic budgets, my office is now analyzing the utilization of academic staff, in what might be called Phase 1 of our developing

FIGURE 5

NEED FOR EXTENSIVE AND DETAILED PROGRAM COST INFORMATION SYSTEM

PRESENT COST INFORMATION BY ORGANIZATIONAL UNIT

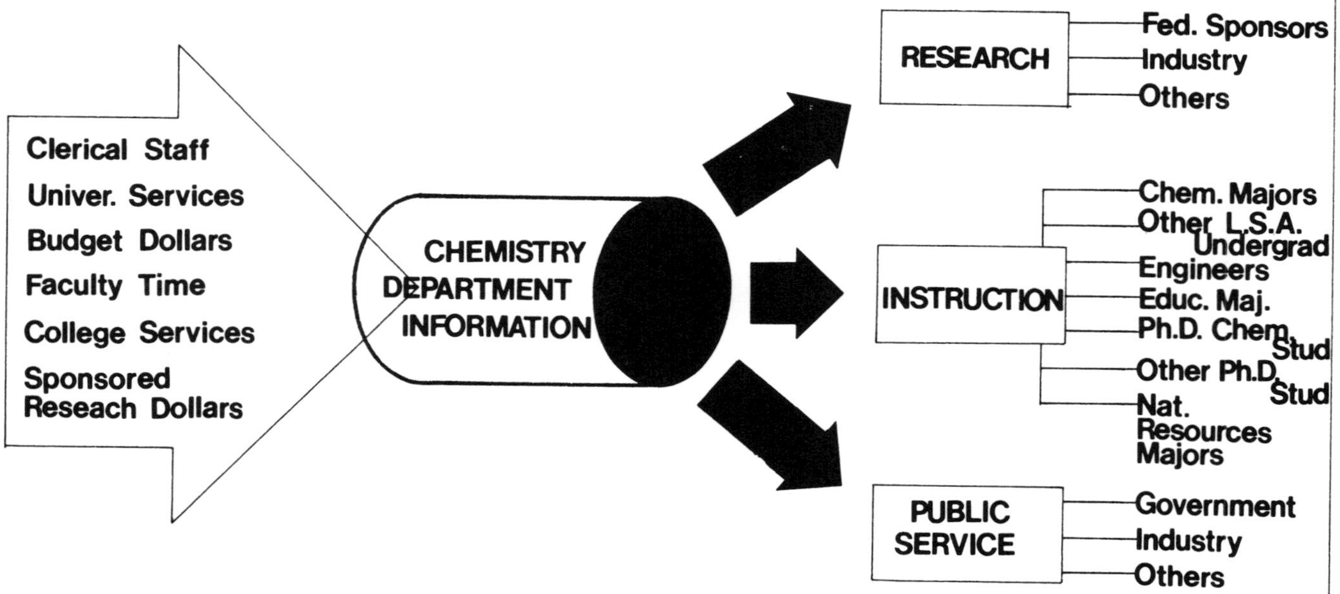

FIGURE 6

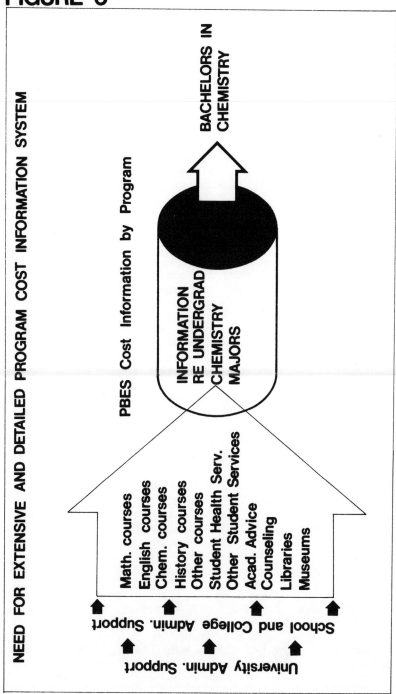

program information system. Unfortunately in the view of many faculty members, a faculty activities report has become one of our basic sources of information. Two other sources are also essential to the system we are building. One is a computerized academic staff file which includes the name, rank, and department of every academic staff member as well as his salary, his fraction of full-time-equivalent appointment and the sources of his salary. The second is a computerized class election file which gives us the college, the academic major, and the level of each student enrolled in every class section. Together then, these sources of information permit us to analyze the utilization of our academic staff in terms of the programs identified by our schools and colleges. It also permits us to identify the contribution of one college or department to the programs of other departments, at least in the area of instruction. Our other two major program categories are research and public service, as one might expect.

At this point I don't want to give you the impression that we have a complete, smoothly functioning programmatic analysis system. We still have many problems, and even Phase 1 has not been completed. Just to give you some idea, the first time we matched our class election file against the class sections which faculty members said they were teaching, we wound up with long lists of classes in which students had registered but which no faculty member claimed he was teaching. We also wound up with long lists of classes which faculty said they were teaching but in which no students were enrolled. For the most part faculty members had put down either the wrong course or the wrong section number on the activities report. But rather than dwell on the mechanical problems we have faced, which I could do all day long, it might be more helpful for our later discussion to identify some of the major issues in PPB Systems, as they apply to colleges and universities.

MAJOR ISSUES

Probably the most widely discussed issue has to do with whether or not the program budgeting approach can be successful in service organizations like colleges and universities. One of the corner stones of the program budget structure is the idea that the resources used will be measured against results achieved. Critics claim that while such a comparison can be made in the production of automobiles, furniture manufacture, or in the garment industry, the outputs of higher education are much more elusive. They further claim that such output units as degrees or student credit hours are very superficial and can mislead budget makers if they are taken too seriously, as providing the only results produced by higher education. This is indeed an old argument about whether and to what extent efficiency can really be accurately measured. My own feeling is that we can do a better job than we have in the past, in measuring the outputs of higher

FIGURE 6

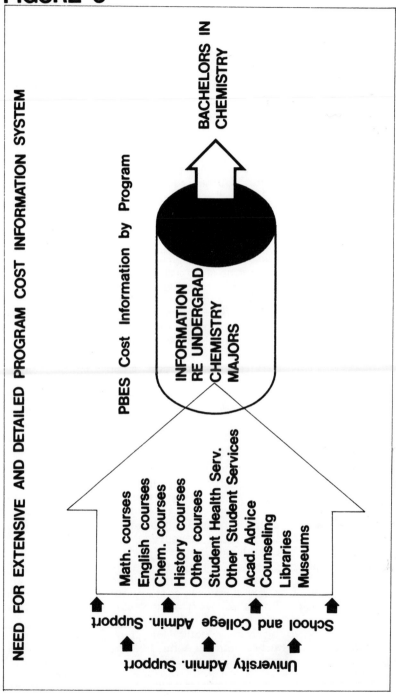

NEED FOR EXTENSIVE AND DETAILED PROGRAM COST INFORMATION SYSTEM

PBES Cost Information by Program

BACHELORS IN CHEMISTRY

INFORMATION RE UNDERGRAD CHEMISTRY MAJORS

Math. courses
English courses
Chem. courses
History courses
Other courses
Student Health Serv.
Other Student Services
Acad. Advice
Counseling
Libraries
Museums

School and College Admin. Support

University Admin. Support

program information system. Unfortunately in the view of many faculty members, a faculty activities report has become one of our basic sources of information. Two other sources are also essential to the system we are building. One is a computerized academic staff file which includes the name, rank, and department of every academic staff member as well as his salary, his fraction of full-time-equivalent appointment and the sources of his salary. The second is a computerized class election file which gives us the college, the academic major, and the level of each student enrolled in every class section. Together then, these sources of information permit us to analyze the utilization of our academic staff in terms of the programs identified by our schools and colleges. It also permits us to identify the contribution of one college or department to the programs of other departments, at least in the area of instruction. Our other two major program categories are research and public service, as one might expect.

At this point I don't want to give you the impression that we have a complete, smoothly functioning programmatic analysis system. We still have many problems, and even Phase 1 has not been completed. Just to give you some idea, the first time we matched our class election file against the class sections which faculty members said they were teaching, we wound up with long lists of classes in which students had registered but which no faculty member claimed he was teaching. We also wound up with long lists of classes which faculty said they were teaching but in which no students were enrolled. For the most part faculty members had put down either the wrong course or the wrong section number on the activities report. But rather than dwell on the mechanical problems we have faced, which I could do all day long, it might be more helpful for our later discussion to identify some of the major issues in PPB Systems, as they apply to colleges and universities.

MAJOR ISSUES

Probably the most widely discussed issue has to do with whether or not the program budgeting approach can be successful in service organizations like colleges and universities. One of the corner stones of the program budget structure is the idea that the resources used will be measured against results achieved. Critics claim that while such a comparison can be made in the production of automobiles, furniture manufacture, or in the garment industry, the outputs of higher education are much more elusive. They further claim that such output units as degrees or student credit hours are very superficial and can mislead budget makers if they are taken too seriously, as providing the only results produced by higher education. This is indeed an old argument about whether and to what extent efficiency can really be accurately measured. My own feeling is that we can do a better job than we have in the past, in measuring the outputs of higher education but that we ought not to become enamored of one or two simplistic measures.

A second and closely related issue has to do with ensuring that various kinds of planning and budgeting decisions are made by those persons who are in the best position to make them. Again, the critics of PPBS claim that all of the analysis and support which generally goes along with the system tends to centralize budget decisions in an uneconomic way. All of the data and plans give the dean the false impression that he understands the problems within a department as well as the department chairman — and so on up the ladder until a state budget officer might get the false feeling that he has sufficient information to make just as good decisions about the internal allocation of university resources as our deans and vice presidents can make. This criticism is potentially valid, but only valid if the concepts are misused. If the dean comes to agreement with the department chairman on the expected **results** of the budget allocation and refrains from deciding **for** the department chairman how he will manage his budget to produce those results, then each manager is making decisions appropriate to his position. However, if planning and program budgeting analyses do not focus on **results,** and if resource allocation decisions are therefore made not on the basis of what is to be accomplished but rather on the basis of less significant considerations such as how many faculty members should be employed and at what rank, then there is a great temptation for higher level administrators to involve themselves in means rather than ends. If they resort to that, then they usurp the managerial prerogatives of others. In the process they also probably make poorer decisions than would be made by the managers who are closer to the actual needs of the specific situation.

A third and more technical issue is another difficult one, and an old one — that is the matter of joint products which result from a single operation or activity. You might recall from your principles course in economics that the production of beef also results in the production of hides, and that it is impossible to get one without the other. This is the joint-product phenomenon, and it describes, of course, many faculty activities. More than that, it describes quite well the major program outputs of higher education. The professor of surgery in performing a new type of operation is rendering a service to the patient, carrying out research, and he might well be instructing other doctors and medical residents simultaneously. How do we budget for that activity in terms of instruction, research, and service programs? By the same token how do we program budget the operating room facilities? Jointness is probably most typical of graduate instruction and research, inasmuch as a great deal of graduate instruction is devoted to training in research methodology.

In fact, most of us would claim, I am sure, that one of the measures of effectiveness and efficiency in a college or university is precisely the extent to which instruction, research, and service programs overlap, thereby yielding multiple or joint products from a single effort. As an illustration, it is quite possible that if we had on the one hand a college with an instructional program only, producing a million dollars worth of instructional service, and a research corporation producing a million dollars worth of research only, and a public service agency producing a million dollars worth of social service, then presumably we would receive three million dollars in value for an expenditure of the same amount. However, if these programs were undertaken by a single organization capable of producing joint products through overlapping activity, then it's quite possible that we would derive three million dollars in value for somewhat lower expenditure, in this illustration 2.4 million dollars. Note that the overlap shown is primarily between graduate instruction and research. At any rate, there appears to be no clearly sensible and acceptable way to account for or budget funds when several different fund sources are financing an activity with joint products. Our funding, budgeting and accounting have to be somewhat arbitrary, even according to the economic literature on the subject.

This conceptual problem seems to apply as much to library services as to some other university activities. To what extent does the cataloging function support the instructional program of an institution, or the research programs, or the public service? Many acquisitions are probably indispensable to good instruction but also serve research and public service purposes. Should the cost of cataloging those volumes be budgeted entirely to instruction because they would have to be incurred whether or not the institution performed research or public service? Or should the costs be split among the three purposes? Even the theoretical economists cannot give us a good answer.

A final issue raised by thorough-going planning and program budgeting has to do with the life style of the academician. When the public was paying a far smaller bill for higher education, there were fewer demands on us to account for what we were doing and what we were producing. Many academic departments were and still are rather loose collections of individuals, and the goals of the department are sometimes as many as there are faculty members in it. It is not too uncommon to find a college which pays little attention to its expert on celestial mechanics who teaches two courses of little interest to students and to other faculty members for that matter. However the notion of program budgeting and accountability implies that the organization itself will have some purposes and that the academic department will have some group objectives and programs. This means that the individual faculty member who has been doing his own thing and has not been closely aligned with departmental programs and purposes might well have a more difficult time in the future justifying his place in the organization. I list this as an important issue because one of the historical precepts to all college and university administrators has been to hire the very best scholared teachers whom they could find and then leave each free to do his own thing.

In higher education we have generally assumed that the best way to discourage a hard working, professional and creative attitude among faculty members would be to tell them precisely what they have to do, and how and when to do it. In this respect, the department chairman can play a crucial role. It is he who will have to serve as a buffer between the managerial requirements imposed by good planning and budgeting on the one hand, and the freedom of the individual faculty member to work most productively and creatively on the other.

Recitation of these issues leads me to my own conclusions about the value of PPBS in higher education, and you might well want to debate these later. Probably the greatest value to be derived lies in the learning which we shall all have to do if we implement such systems. We shall have to dig more deeply than will be comfortable for us into the reasons why we currently manage our resources the way we do. We shall have to articulate in much more concrete terms than we ever have before precisely what we expect to accomplish. We shall have to dig out a lot more information then we ever have about the nature of our current enterprise. Having done all of this, the masses of data generated will be much less important in our planning and budgeting then they appear to be at first. We shall be better able to put the numbers in perspective and hopefully will have established the habit of more thoughtful and thorough consideration in planning and carrying out our responsibilities. This appears to be the experience of the federal government, which evidently is currently dismantling at least part of its PPBS effort. It is retaining, however, the practice of generating reports on critical program issues which have important budget implications. In that aspect of the system, program budget analysts put into writing the crucial problems, federal agency by federal agency, which provide background information for budget discussions and negotiations with each agency.

———

THE EFFECTIVE USE OF PPBS
TO IMPROVE LIBRARY MANAGEMENT

Harold R. Jenkins

Director, Lancastor County Library
Lancastor, Pennsylvania

There are converts to the use of the management technique called PPBS (Planning, Programming, Budgeting System) who speak about their newly acquired knowledge with a sense of reverence and solemn wonder. They have some of the appearance of fanatics going about with their arms uplifted, singing praises to Program Memoranda, Program Structures, Program Financial Plans and Program Evaluation as though this administrative procedure will provide a panacea for all the ills of the business world.

Let me hasten to say that we are not working with the supernatural when we apply the principles of PPB. It is great. It has fantastic possibilities. But after all, it is only a management concept — an organized, disciplined way of thinking about the things we do. It is a technique, a concept, a philosophy — call it what you will — that successful administrators have been using for many years as they have gone about their tasks of making decisions.

An understanding of the process of making decisions and of the role of the manager as a decision-maker should be thoroughly comprehended at this point in our discussion before we move on to the practical application of PPB to the decision-making process.

C. W. Churchman said: "The manager is the man who decides among alternative choices. He must decide which choice he believes will lead to a certain desired objective or set of objectives".[1] Samuel Eilon pointed out that "The essential ingredients in this definition are that the decision-maker has **several alternatives** and that his choice involves a **comparison** between these alternatives and the **evaluation of their outcomes**".[2]

Over the years many systems have been devised to aid in decision-making. For the most part they all encourage the manager to identify the problem, to gather facts, to consider alternatives, and then to decide which course of action he will follow. It has been said that the decision process starts with an information input.[3] The real beginning, however, starts with conceptualizing an idea or with recognizing that a problem exists. Otherwise everything works along very nicely and no structured decisions are required.

Samuel Eilon has also pointed out that rational behavior is required on the part of the decision-maker.[4] This is to say that when a decision is made, the steps leading to that decision should follow a logical development based on the inputs that are provided in the initial study. The Eilon point of view about rationality in decision-making presents a highly structured process that closely resembles the routine of finding an answer from a series of imputs that are lined up and added like a column of figures.

This point of view is somewhat tempered with the understanding that under certain circumstances a degree of initiative or freedom of choice may be allowed to the decision-maker. At one extreme in the decision-making process we have "random control" and at the other "Impersonalistic-formal control".[5]

Those who have made studies of decision-making can show that "Starting with a situation in which decisions and corrective actions are taken in a haphazard fashion (random control) in the absence of any directives, an individual emerges and tries to regularize these actions and mould them into a systematic and consistent pattern".[6]

I understand this statement to mean that the art of decision-making follows an evolutionary development running from off-the-cuff decisions based on a random sampling of inputs or no inputs to the more sophisticated decision-making that tends to become independent of the emotions of an individual. All managers and managerial processes are to be found somewhere between these two extremes.

A word of caution at this point. I do not wish to convey the thought that a decision based on a random sampling of inputs is automatically less valid than a decision based on every conceivable input. Take for example this thing we call intuition. It can play a role in the scheme of things.

Isabel Rockowner writing in the March 1970 issue of **Supervisory Management**,[7] said this about intuition:

"In deciding on some matters, you have to rely largely on your instincts. In making an intuitive decision, you consider all the available facts, but instead of deciding solely on rational grounds, you let your feelings influence the way you interpret the facts.

"The difficulty, says one psychologist, is that many people block off their feelings so that their real wants don't surface. The acid test is how satisfied you are with a decision you've made. If you feel uneasy, chances are that you either ignored your feelings or had no confidence in them. When that happens, experts advise, stop trying to be rational. Scrap the decision and do what you feel is right."

Now we have arrived at a natural point where we should discuss the ability of individuals to make decisions that will lead to the achievement of a recognized goal. We all understand that there is no equality in ability. Our power to decide is something that each of us has in varying degrees. "What one man can do is not necessarily what another can do. What we can do in one situation may be different from what we can accomplish in another".[8]

Thus far we have been giving attention to the decision-making process itself and to the relative abilities of individuals to arrive at rational decisions. Let us take this same information and put it in the hands of someone called a manager. A manager is a decision-maker. "A manager's primary tasks are policy making, major problem solving, and creative planning."[9] Above all the manager makes decisions.

From our discussion we have been reminded that the process of decision-making can result from a purely intuitive response to a given situation where man is still in control. At the other end of the spectrum decision-making can be the final step in a chain of sequential activities that run from the statement of a problem through the gathering of information, through the analysis of the information, to the building of alternate approaches that describe how the problem might be solved to measures of performance for each of the alternate approaches and finally to the decision itself.[10]

The variables in this process of decision-making are infinite. In many ways one can liken management to the presentation of a musical thought. Like the composer who can take a musical thought and present it in new and varied aspects, yet keeping the essential features of the original idea true to the original theme, the manager can move toward a goal, toward an ultimate objective, using his own special mix of people, materials and money and yet not stray from the original purpose.

As long as people manage and make decisions the end results are going to be different. At the extreme end of this decision-making process, when control becomes divorced from the influence of people through computerization, the decision, the manager as we are thinking of him today, will cease to play a meaningful role. Until that day arrives man the manager will continue to exert his influence from the point where the problem is introduced to its final solution.

Thus far we have touched briefly on the process of making decisions. We have identified the manager as a decision-maker. It is still essential before we get down to the point of discussing PPB to consider the role that a manager plays in the decision-making process. It may be well to define the term management itself.

According to Webster, management is "the judicious use of means to accomplish an end." If we substitute the term "administration" for "management" we can turn to the **International Encyclopedia of the Social Sciences** for guidance. Under the heading "The Administrative Function" we find this definition: [11]

"...administration is a process of arriving at decisions operationally homologous to other decision-making processes in large-scale organizations, and that the importance of administration lies not in the uniqueness of its function but in the increasing prominence of administrators as compared to other participants in the making of decisions."

Now we have established that as a manager, as an administrator, you are important in the scheme of things. You are not just a cog in the wheel. You are the wheel. It has been accepted for a long time that a cog is a person functioning as part of a process or organization. The wheel is considered to be the moving power.

We have established that the decision-making process has infinite variety; that man the manager may well be a wheel, but he is not a machine. It follows that when you accept the responsibility of being a manager, you had better learn to scramble, to live by your wits, to make decisions that count. In the final analysis no matter how you manage to spread responsibility among all those cogs on that wheel of yours, you're it.

I have provided this background for our discussion of PPBS because I think it is essential that those who are moving into management positions should understand that there is no one magic formula that will guarantee success. Training for management is a lifetime operation that should have begun while you were a kid in grade school. Like musicians who begin in their childhood to learn the lines and spaces, you should have begun as a child to prepare for management by first learning how to get along with other people. You should have learned through your years in school how to evaluate your teachers, how to organize your thought processes, how to make things happen so they came out the way you wanted them to come out.

Your first lessons in major decision-making should have begun in your young adult years, especially as you began to give systematic thought to making plans for your future. You may have learned then to set down your goal or objective in writing and to line up the arguments for and against taking a particular course of action.

You decided what you wanted to do and why you wanted to do it — and you put those decisions in writing. You next lined up a number of ways of doing the things you wanted to do and, choosing one of these ways, you put that way in writing.

Recognizing that everything has a cost in money or time or energy expended, you then defined the costs for any one decision-making situation and put them in writing. It follows that there was only so much money or time or energy available to do the many things you wanted to do, so you fed the figures from each of your decision-making situations into a column of figures that you then added up to find a total for all your projected activities.

Following this you took the amount of money, time or energy that you could count on to do the things you wanted to do and compared those resources with your anticipated wants or expenditures. If the expenditures were greater than the resources, you either added to the resources or subtracted from the activities. At any rate, the availability of money, time or energy had to balance with the plans to spend that money, time or energy.

That, in its simplest possible terms, is Planning, Programming, Budgeting. You can wrap PPB up in all sorts of definitions such as:

"...a methodology for organizing information to improve decisions having to do with the allocation of resources."

or "...a system aimed at helping management make better decisions on the allocation of resources among alternative ways to attain ... objectives."

or "...PPBS is a system of relating planning to budgeting that seeks to get your dollars worth for you by analyzing what you are doing in light of what you should be doing and plan to do in the years to come and tying that back to your standard yearly budget".[12]

There is a major difference, however, between PPB and the decision-making process where a choice is made from a number of alternative ways of achieving a nearby objective. The difference is not in the individual decision-making technique used in the modern planning, programming, budgeting concept. This technique is no different from that which has always been used. The problem is identified; information is gathered and analysed; alternative ways of solving the problem are proposed and finally the decision-maker makes a selection from the several alternatives.

The difference lies in the concept that PPB is a system approach to achieving an ultimate objective.

This means that beside weighing the relative value of one way over another to achieve a nearby objective, you now begin to think in terms of how that nearby objective contributes to the process of achieving your ultimate objective. You are searching for alternate ways of doing things or in demanding that the item you are paying for buy some future value.[13]

We are now ready to go to work, to develop a PPBS model that can be applied to your particular situation. It doesn't make any difference what your situation happens to be, the model can be applied. You may be the manager of a business — large or small, or a library, or a hospital, or a large university. It is all the same as far as the concept of PPBS is concerned. In each case you have an ultimate objective that you hope to achieve by making proper decisions as you move along through the years.

CONSTRUCTING A PPBS MODEL

First: State your ultimate objective, your reason for being in business.

Second: Identify your basic programs or functions.

Third: Subdivide these basic programs or functions so that each activity making up your total operation is visible.

Fourth: Define each sub-program as follows:
a. Make a simple statement of **why** you do what you **want** to do and **where** you want to do it.
b. Make another simple statement telling **how** to do **what** you want to do.
c. Make a statement of the costs in money, time or energy to carry out each sub-program.

Fifth: Carry the totals for each identifiable cost within each sub-program to its appropriate **Administrative** sub-program.

Sixth: Carry the totals for each identifiable cost within each sub-program to a line budget.

Seventh: Total all line items on the expense side of the budget and compare this figure with the total line items on the income side. If the balance is not satisfactory or if for any reason dissatisfaction is expressed about the expenditures, return to the appropriate sub-program or sub-programs to reexamine the questioned expenditure in the light of its value as a contribution to the success of the sub-program.

Eight: Set up a methodology for evaluating the effectiveness of each sub-program as that sub-program relates to the ultimate goal.

It would be well to note that all planning, programming, budgeting statements should be made without becoming involved in jargon or convoluted sentences. In all cases the programs should be written in simple, straight forward words and phrases that can be easily understood. Part of the value of the PPBS concept is that it provides a means whereby the manager may communicate with the members of his staff as well as with the members of his board of directors. It is this communication, this understanding of the overall program by all levels of management that separates PPB budgeting from traditional budgeting.

Before we get down to looking at an actual plan to implement PPBS, I should like to suggest that there is some danger in carrying the explanation of the PPBS model beyond the brief summary given above. One danger is that one man's budget could be another man's poison.

This type of planning can only be effective if it is developed and carried out by a management team that has the ability to think creatively about the relationship between its product, its resources and its ultimate goal. A manager with imagination can conceptualize an idea. He can see the full form of an idea in his mind's eye. Seeing the idea fully formed, he can then manage his resources so that he will take effective steps toward realizing his goal. Those steps should require easy communication with all levels of his management team. This is where PPBS comes into play.

The decision-making technique in a one-man operation follows the same pattern as that discussed earlier in this paper. However, the process need not be visible as it is in the PPBS process because all elements of the one-man program are controlled by the decision-maker himself. He doesn't have to write out the "what" and "why" and "how" for any one's benefit except his own. And that writing need be done only for purposes of clarifying his thinking — not to communicate with others.

The decision-maker in a multi-level administrative setup needs the support of his staff, the approval of his board or whatever his governing body may be called, as well as reasonable understanding on the part of those who allocate funds. The decision-maker realizes the value of involving people at all levels. For example, department heads who carry out the details of his programs should help to plan those programs. They should also understand the relationship of cost to performance. On the other hand, board members as well as those authorities who allocate funds should be able to see evidence in the current year budget of values being added to the operation that will, to the extent of those values, carry the operation closer to its ultimate goal.

EXAMPLE OF THE PPBS MODEL:

Situation: You have taken over the management of a public library serving a city and county area. Your library has been in business for many years. For the most part the pattern of approving annual budgets has been one of following a fiscal policy set in the early 1800's, a policy that is best summarized in this statement made by one of the early librarians: "It must be very apparent how this library has been enabled to prolong its existence and usefulness for more than half a century, namely, by keeping intact its invested funds, and economically confining its expenditures within the limits of its income from accruing interest and subscription to the library." The limitation expressed here of "economically confining its expenditures **within the limits of its income...**" would immediately kill any possibility of promoting a long-range program. Long-range programs require acceptance that the direction in which you are moving is quite proper and worth working toward. To achieve this level of understanding you must define your long-range program in terms that will be understood by your staff as well as by your superiors. Having gained acceptance for your long-range program, you then come to terms with implementing that program within the framework of available funds.

Certainly I am not proposing deficit spending. Simply because plans have been proposed that call for funding beyond the level of foreseeable income does not require actual expenditures beyond that level. You have simply raised the sights of those who appropriate funds so they can see where you are going.

Having made these explanatory comments we can now proceed with an example of the PPBS model.

First Step: Define your ultimate objective.
Example: To provide quality library service to meet the needs of all the citizens of the county at the lowest dollar cost.

Second Step: Identify the basic functions.
Example:
1. Library materials
2. Cooperative efforts
3. Working with independent libraries
4. Extending service
5. Communication
6. Administration

In a narrative statement the above functions would be grouped as follows:

Point 1: The public library in our problem situation provides its service through the provision of library materials — books, films, periodicals, maps, etc.

Point 2: In its efforts to provide effective service the management of the library seeks assistance outside its immediate administrative area in the form of cooperation with other libraries, cooperation with non-library agencies as well as cooperation with individuals.

Point 3: The management has noted that there are many small independent public libraries in the area served by the county library. It has been determined that these independent librarians should be drawn into a system arrangement without denying them the opportunity to operate as autonomous units.

Point 4: An interest is also shown in extending library service to all areas of the county — to nursing homes, county prison, one room schools, as well as to communities now presently served by independent libraries.

Point 5: The manager also realizes the need to have a public relations program, to make effective use of the mails, telephone, teletype, television, vehicle delivery service.

Point 6: All of these functions — library materials, cooperative efforts, working with independent libraries, extending service as well as communication — are tied together in another basic function called administration.

Encompassing statements will be needed for each of the basic functions. These statements should be brief, to the point but not restrictive. For instance, regarding the extension of service to other areas of the county, the manager could make the following initial statement:

Sub-Function: Extension Service:

"The overall plan for extending the library program throughout the county calls for the provisions of outreach service designed to meet the needs of all citizens. This means that programs will be enlarged — limited only by money, imagination and need — to the point where library service is brought within the reach of all citizens. The program will be developed to a point of excellence where it will not be necessary for a user from any part of the county to make direct use of the headquarters library unless he desires to do so.

"This phase of the program will depend upon interest generated in each local community or neighborhood of the larger cities within the county. The strength of the outreach program rests with the degree of interest shown by the local group. If it is judged that sufficient interest has been generated, the headquarters library will establish an outlet in the area.

"In following this course of action, the Administration of the headquarters library will encourage the local group to understand that its outlet — whatever its size — is an important part of the total library system. Therefore, the members of the local interest group assume a share of the responsibility for encouraging the proper authorities to give adequate financial support to the total library program."

Perhaps it would be well to give one more example that will show how the basic functions should be stated so that they cover the fundamental philosophy without imposing arbitrary limits that would interfere with creative management.

SECOND EXAMPLE:

Function: Administration.

Statement: All administrative procedures of the library have been placed under a system of continuous revision leading to maximum service at the lowest possible cost. The establishment of new administrative procedures will be guided by the need to have the county library become the focal point for all recreational, informational and educational reading requests directed to the library by all the citizens of the county. Identifying the administrative setup of the library — or any business — as a separate function will allow the manager to overcome a difficulty that has been experienced in the development of PPB systems among federal agencies. The problem at that level has been one of integrating the PPB system with the related systems of financial management and the budgetary process.

We can relate this same situation to integrating our PPB system for this problem with the conventional administrative organization of our library where personnel functions are seen in relationship to departments within the library. There is no need to recognize the administrative operation in order to carry out the concept of PPB. We get around this problem by considering administration as one of the basic functions of the operation that accounts for the **time** of its personnel. The **work** that is accomplished by one's staff is then covered by the other basic functions, i. e., selecting books under Point 1; setting up library centers in the smaller communities under Point 5.

Third Step: Subdividing basic functions so that each activity making up the total operation is visible.

Example: Under the basic function of Point 4, Extension Service, we find the following sub-functions:
1. Service to nursing homes
2. Service to one room schools
3. Service to the inner-city
4. Service to handicapped
5. Service to the county prison
6. Other areas of outreach service including bookmobile service.

EXAMPLE: Subdividing the activities under the basic function of Point 6, Administration. Among these sub-functions you will find the organization of various departments such as "Extension", "Reference", "Cataloging", Children's plus any other activity that involves people and/or services that do not belong in the other five basic program areas. This means that to the sub-functions or activities listed above we can add "Annual Book Sale", "In-service Training", "Building Maintenance", "Volunteer Service," "Use of IBM automatic typewriters", "Photocopying", and so forth.

This subdividing of the basic functions continues until you have accounted for each activity that is important enough to deserve the visibility that it will be given through such a listing.

Fourth Step: Define each sub-program.

For the purpose of this example, we will take one sub-program under the major function "Extension" and one from the major function "Administration". It is in writing the definition of each of the sub-programs that the manager gets into the heart of the PPB system. He has established his long-range objective, set-up his basic programs and divided these into their appropriate activities or sub-programs. Now he sets forth in writing "why" he does "what" he wants to do, "how" he is going to do it and then a statement about the cost.

At this point the manager may introduce three terms that have come into current use as a result of this PPB line of thinking. These terms are:

a. Program Memorandum
b. Program Structure
c. Program Financial Plan

These are fairly descriptive words that can be used to some advantage. The "Program Memorandum" is a statement in simple words and phrases that sets forth what the manager wants to do and why he wants to do it. The following represents an example of a Program Memorandum under the basic function Point 4, Extension Service.

Program Memorandum:
No: 4A

Subject: Service to the disadvantaged in the inner-city area.

Statement: The library recognizes the need and actual hunger for library service among the disadvantaged citizens of the inner-city area. However, the majority of these people themselves do not know what it is they need, why they need it or where they can find what they are looking for when they do understand their need. The main library is a short distance in miles from the people but endlessly distant because of the cultural and economic lag that exist in many areas of the city. The latter is a problem for the sociologists; but the problem of providing every possible avenue for learning, for pleasure and for growth in cultural pride lies squarely in the lap of the management of the library. Accordingly, our program will be one of carrying the message of library service to these people.

You will note that we have remained with our resolve to say only that which had to be said in giving the "what" and "why" for this particular program. It is at this point that we get into the endless business of determining whether or not a particular sub-program is a proper extension of one of the basic programs. It is presumed, of course, that your basic programs have been endorsed by proper authority; i. e., your charter of incorporation, your appointing authority, whatever.

As an indication of the value of words, you will note in the last sentence of the Program Memorandum we have said that "our program will be one of carrying the **message** of library service...". This does not place a demand on the central library to establish branch service — or any library service, for that matter. This type of flexibility must be allowed by your program memorandum or you will find yourself boxed in. Remember, the program memorandum gives you the "what and the "why". However, it does not become involved in the "how".

It should be obvious that after you have stated your problem — in this case a recognition of the need to carry the message of library service to the disadvantaged of the inner-city — you will then consider various alternate solutions to the problem. From these two, three or more possible ways of solving your problem you will finally choose one that appears to meet your needs most effectively. Having made this decision, you will now begin to prepare another statement — again in simple, easily understood phrases — describing how you are going to do what you want to do. This second type of statement is called the "Program Structure".

The following represents an example of a program structure. For this purpose we will follow through with Point 4, Extension Service and the sub-function "Service to the disadvantaged in the inner-city area".

Program Structure.
No. 4AA

Subject: Service to the disadvantaged in the inner-city area.

Statement: Having determined that our program is one of carrying the message of library service to the disadvantaged of the inner-city, and also having determined that this message is one concerned with the provision of library material and service relating to information, education and recreation, we have concluded that the best way to carry this message would seem to be by setting up a temporary base in the form of a trailer library from which the outreach program can be carried on. The trailer will be staffed by a professional librarian having special training in service to the disadvantaged, two assistants from the larger ethnic groups — Black and Spanish, and one clerk. To facilitate their work we will provide a general collection of books plus special collections of Black and Spanish literature. To promote mobility we will need a van that will make it possible for the staff to reach all cummunities in the area. In addition, there will be a motion picture projector, filmstrip projector, amplifying equipment, book racks, book bags, telephone, electrical service as well as insurance. It should also be noted that this will be a continuing program that will require support on an annual, recurring basis.

You will note that the structure has been formed so that it will reflect all costs involved in carrying out the full purpose set forth in the program memorandum allied to it. Although the structure explains how a particular idea may be implemented, it is not detailed or quantified to the extent that it will prescribe the manner in which the various ingredients of staff, equipment and library material will be combined to carry out the purpose set forth in the program memorandum.

The "Program Financial Plan" should define estimated or actual costs as they have been outlined in the program structure.

Such costs may be divided into three major categories:

a. Direct costs, including labor and material,
b. Shared costs, including labor and material,
c. Initiating expense and/or other non-recurring cost.

"Direct" costs are those that are primarily consumed by the program itself. Such costs could include personnel, equipment and supplies as such items are used up by the program.

"Shared" costs are just that — costs for labor or material that are not entirely consumed by one program.

For instance, the supervisor of the Extension Service Department spends her time looking after many different programs. In each of these programs her time is listed as a shared cost. In a similar way the driver of a local delivery service will have his time divided between all of the areas he serves. His time will be noted as a shared cost on many different programs. On the other hand, a staff member who spends her full time operating within a particular program will have her full time recorded as a direct cost to that program.

In truth, this is the beginning of cost accounting. You divide your entire operation into activities than can be seen, understood and analyzed for cost purposes. Although we will want to give further consideration to the role that cost accounting plays in the PPB structure, my immediate concern at this moment is to show an example of one way a program financial plan can be worked out.

It is at this point in the development of the PPB technique that we can see how each individual program can be made to blend with all other programs. Once a program has been spelled out in terms of money, another discipline comes into play. I refer to accounting or perhaps to a larger concept — budgetary control.

We know that "a budget is a plan for future events and courses of action that is stated in money terms".[14] Also, according to one introductory text on cost accounting, "a budget is a **gross** plan in the sense that it summarizes many detailed estimates and decisions about a variety of future actions and events",[15] It follows that the only sensible way that we can hope to make "estimates and decisions about a variety of future actions" is by being able to see the **inter-relationship** of those future actions **in the light of the goal that those actions are designed to help us achieve.** This is what budgetary control is about.

It should be obvious that the figures produced through each program financial plan must join similar figures from other programs. Otherwise it will not be posible to study the inter-relationship of the proposed future plans and to come to a decision regarding the implementation or modification of such plans.

As we look at our example of a Program Financial Plan, we

can see through the following explanation how these figures can begin to play an active part in the larger decision-making process.

These figures are simply transferred to an appropriate sub-program or sub-programs within the basic function we have called Point 6, Administration. There they will join other figures from all other activities or sub-programs. In accounting terms this process may be referred to as the assembly and analysis of pertinent data that in turn is designed to give an overall view or forecast of an entire activity for the budget period.[16]

You will recall that we have already discussed the merit of identifying the administration of an organization as one of the basic functions; that in so doing you will overcome a difficulty that has been experienced in the development of PPB systems among federal agencies. The problem apparently has been one of trying to structure administrative organizations along the functional lines set forth as a base for their PPB system. In other words, departmentalization has apparently given way to organizing according to functions. This is not necessary nor, in my opinion, wise to do.

The fact is that this is one of the beauties of PPBS. You don't have to reorganize in any sense of the word. All interrelationships of people may remain as they were set up before planning, programming and budgeting came on the scene. The difference will be that the people will understand why they are doing what they are doing, and they also know how their particular operations contribute to an ultimate goal.

I have one note of caution to add at this point before we carry on with the explanation of how these figures may be transferred to appropriate administrative sub-programs. We are beginning to talk about accounting. This is a discipline of its own. If you are part of a university or school system or industrial complex, the accounting procedures will be prescribed for you. However, this does not mean that such procedures will keep you from practicing the **principles** of planning, programming and budgeting. These two techniques are not mutually exclusive; instead they are mutually supportive.

Now we can get back to the figures in the program financial plan shown in our example. You will note immediately that the personnel figures are given in hours of work. The actual money value for those hours will be shown when those figures are transferred to the appropriate sub-program under the basic function "Administration". This thinking is based on the understanding that the people involved in a budgeting activity should also be involved in the preparation of the budget.

It follows that the department heads preparing the program memorandum, program structure and program financial plan are

PROGRAM FINANCIAL PLAN   Date_____

NO: 4AAA

SUBJECT: Service to the disadvantaged in the inner-city area.

Recurring Costs:	First Year		Second Year		Third Year	
	Hrs.	$	Hrs.	$	Hrs.	$
Direct:						
Personnel:						
a. Professional Supervisor	40		40		40	
b. Library Assistant, Black	40		40		40	
c. Library Assistant, Spanish	40		40		40	
d. Clerk	20		20		20	
Library Materials:						
a. Books		3,000		3,000		4,000
b. Periodicals		200		200		250
c. Audio-Visual		300		300		300
Utilities:						
a. Telephone		100		100		120
b. Electricity		1,000		1,000		1,100
c. Water		50		50		50
Miscellaneous:						
a. Vehicle Maintenance		300		300		300
b. Travel		200		200		200
c. Supplies		100		100		100
d. Insurance		400		400		400
Shared Costs:						
Personnel:						
a. Extension Supervisor	15		10		10	
b. Delivery Service Driver	4		4		4	
c. Other						
Total Recurring Costs:	159	$5,650	154	$5,650	154	$6,845

	First Year	Second Year	Third Year

Non-recurring Costs:

    (To include initiating costs
    as well as capital improvements)

    Equipment:

		First Year	Second Year	Third Year
a.	Library Trailer	$24,000	$ -0-	$ -0-
b.	Filmstrip Projectors	80	-0-	-0-
c.	16mm Projector	650	-0-	-0-
d.	Screen	100	-0-	-0-
e.	Van-type Vehicle	3,000	-0-	-0-
f.	Generator	200	-0-	-0-
g.	Amplification Equipment	350	-0-	-0-

    Library Materials:

		First Year	Second Year	Third Year
a.	Books	7,000	(See recurring costs above)	
b.	Filmstrips	200	"_____"	"_____"

Total Non-recurring Costs:	$35,560	-0-	-0-

primarily interested in allocating time when they think in terms of using people. Generally only the main office knows the various levels of pay among the members of the staff.

It also follows somewhat logically that in the initial preparation of the financial plan for a specific activity, the department head preparing that plan could show the number of titles of books, of periodicals, of filmstrips, etc. rather than a dollar figure for these same categories. However, for our example we have shown hours for personnel and dollar figures for all other times. The transfers to the next higher level may be made as follows:

Each line item in a financial plan for an activity will be transferred to a corresponding line item in the appropriate administrative sub-program. (See example, p. 43)

Perhaps it would be well at this point to carry this example one step further in order to show the final outcome — the annual line budget. According to the procedure I have recommended in this instance, specific line items are identified during the early preparation of the budget. However, when the item is finally transferred to the line budget, only general categories such as Library Materials, Library Equipment, etc, are shown. Nicely enough, each of these general categories can be traced back to the original costs as they are shown in the PPB set up.

As I have already said, this process of gathering together the costs for all the activities within a function is known in accounting terms as "the assembly and analysis of various estimates that in turn are designed to give an overall forecast of the entire activity for the budget period. This is one more way of saying that having selected an ultimate objective, having identified all the basic functions and having delineated all the activities that make up each of the functions, you finally summarize your entire operation in terms of dollars and cents. This final summary is called the annual line budget. (See example, p. 44)

We have seen that planning, programming and budgeting involves three concepts or disciplined ways of looking at things. They are decision-making, accounting, evaluation. Each of these disciplines has its own group of supporters or specialists. Evaluators have their way of looking at the world; accountants, their way. The manager is not a specialist in either of these areas. Still he must identify his problem, set up alternative ways of solving that problem, consider the relative values of each of the ways and then establish budgetary control through the use of accounting procedures.

Thus far I have directed your attention to the role of the manager as a decision-maker and as an accountant. The eighth point in the model showing how a PPB system is constructed referred to the need to "set up a methodology for evaluating the

PROGRAM FINANCIAL PLAN

NO: 6-1-AAA

SUBJECT: The Administration of Extension Service

Recurring Costs:

	First Year	Second Year	Third Year	Fourth Year
Direct:				

Personnel:

a.	Salaries	$ 40,451
b.	Social Security	2,184
c.	Retirement	2,023
d.	Hospitalization	336
e.	Unemployment Compensation	180

Library Materials:

a.	Books	11,000
b.	Periodicals	800
c.	Audio-Visual	500

Utilities:

a.	Telephone	300
b.	Electricity	1,000
c.	Water	50

Miscellaneous:

a.	Vehicle Maintenance	450
b.	Travel	400
c.	Supplies	200
d.	Insurance	550

Total Recurring Costs: $ 60,424

Non-recurring Costs:

Equipment:

a.	All weather book return boxes	$ 200
b.	Library Trailer	24,000
c.	Filmstrip Projectors	120
d.	16mm Projector	650
e.	Screen	100
f.	Van-type Vehicle	3,000
g.	Generator	200
h.	Amplification Equipment	350
i.	Shelving	600

Library Materials:

a.	Books	7,000
b.	Filmstrips	200

Total Non-recurring Costs: $ 36,420

Figures for second, third, fourth and subsequent year programs are drawn from appropriate financial plans. You will note that this particular plan summarizes all of the costs that in turn have been worked out in detail through the numerous financial plans covering activities that make up the work of Extension Service.

For our example we have shown only one financial plan for an activity. It should be remembered that there must be financial plans for service to industry, to nursing homes, to schools, to library centers, as well as for bookmobile service.

ANNUAL LINE BUDGET

LIBRARY XYZ

Recurring Costs:

Personnel:

a.	Salaries	$ 219,290
b.	Social Security	11,225
c.	Retirement	8,810
d.	Hospitalization	2,338
e.	Unemployment Compensation	1,500

Library Materials:

a.	Books	98,400
b.	Periodicals	12,000
c.	Audio-Visual	3,000
d.	Microfilm	5,000

Building and Grounds:

a.	Electricity	7,400
b.	Fuel	3,000
c.	Gas and Water	275
d.	Elevator Inspection	1,000
e.	Insurance	3,000
f.	Building Security	4,700
g.	Building Supplies	700

Miscellaneous:

a.	Bookmobile and Delivery Service	3,000
b.	Treasurer's Fee	1,200
c.	Travel	1,600
d.	Membership fee	750

Equipment and Supplies:

a.	Library Supplies	8,000
b.	Postage	2,000

Total Recurring Costs: $ 398,188

Non-recurring Costs:

a.	Library Equipment	$ 43,000
b.	Library Materials	22,000

Total Non-recurring Costs: $ 65,000

Remarks:

All the items in the annual line budget are drawn from program financial plans similar to the example shown on page 5 of this OUTLINE AND GUIDE.

Although it is not shown in this example, the annual budget must offer an overview of the cost to operate four, five or more years into the future. This is accomplished by simply requiring that all sub-functions or sub-programs include such anticipated costs in their projections.

effectiveness of each sub-program as that sub-program relates to the ultimate goal".

Evaluation plays a very important part in PPB systems. Every technique known to management as well as techniques that remain to be developed must be applied at one time or another to weighing the value of a particular decision as that decision in turn affects the ultimate outcome of the total program. One effective source of an on the spot evaluation can be found in the members of the staff who have helped to create the program and who, in turn, should be held responsible for seeing to it that their programs make an honest contribution toward reaching the ultimate goal. It is quite valid to accept as **one** input an expression of approval or disapproval that is based on an intuitive feeling. No facts. No statistics. Just a feeling that may, when viewed in a softer light, be referred to as an "educated guess" or "estimate".

It would be well, too, if the manager were to move to a new plateau regarding his understanding of the role of statistics as a measure of library service. David Palmer, Head of Reader Services, the New Jersey State Library, pointed the way toward this new plateau in a paper presented at an Institute On Program Planning and Budgeting Systems for Libraries, held at Wayne State University in 1968. Briefly, his observations and recommendations ran as follows: [17]

"For the purposes of PPBS, don't rely on statistics which are designed to compare your library with another library."

"Be prepared to keep any counts whatsoever, whether scoffed at by the profession or not, if they can assist you in this comparison."

"Do not hesitate to use sampling techniques, and don't hesitate to ask for expert help in designing a sample which is defensible and illustrative."

"Don't expect the American Library Association to solve all your statistical dilemmas."

"Only you can determine what it is you need to measure to satisfy the data demands of a program-planning and budgeting system."

"Never assume that quantitative data cannot be gathered to illustrate qualitative output."

"Reach out for help from experts who deal with the problems our work touches upon. They will be complimented, and we will be praised for our good jugement in coming to them."

We should expand on David Palmer's recommendation that we reach out for help from experts. Here he was thinking in terms of people as experts. There is another source of expertise that is immediately available to all library managers. I refer to the wealth of information on all aspects of management contained in those thousands of articles to be found in our periodical collections.

Take the November 1971 issue of "Management Accounting" for example. From the point of view of a manager there are a number of excellent articles that will provide significant help in many situations. To prove my point, stay with me for a few minutes while I quote at random from eight different articles contained in one slim issue of this magazine.

"Historically, we accountants have accepted, with some pride, our role as financial custodians. ...Surely it must be our proclivity for accuracy and our preoccupation with balance that gives rise to the financial "policeman" image with which we must live." [18]

COMMENT: Isn't that how we think of accountants. And doesn't that image affect our understanding of the role of accounting in PPB systems? Isn't it interesting to note that accountants also have that their problems with their public image.

"One picture is worth a thousand words in explaining the cost of operations to employees ... Making accounting information a part of the employee information system has had a stimulating effect on employee performance." [19]

COMMENT: Doesn't that stir your imagination? Have you thought very much about involving all of your employees in the actual budgeting process? PPB will help you do this.

"The accounting profession faces the rather formidable task of breaking out of its own 'shell' and providing all management levels with the necessary information for decision-making." [20]

COMMENT: That's exciting news! Now we know that we are not alone. The accounting profession wants to help us evaluate our programs.

"Human assets are the most important single key to the future profitability and success of any business enterprise." [21]

COMMENT: Surely we do not dispute this observation. But a question should be asked: How well do we train our employees? How effectively do we appoint key members to our management team?

"The central authority of the firm (substitute "Library") must provide the lower echelons of management with workable guidelines that will allow them to submit logical project requests." [22]

COMMENT: Again, isn't that a function of PPBS?

"It appears the 'intuition' approach based on the decision-maker's judgment and experience is still a very necessary and important step in finding the correct decision." [23]

COMMENT: Didn't I tell you so?

"Accounting for human resources is part of a new concept of management." [24]

COMMENT: A new concept? I can hardly believe it.

It should be clear that this paper alone cannot be expected to touch on all areas of management with equal facility and enlightenment. My purpose has been to clear the air, to stir the imagination if possible and to set the scene so that those reading this paper or hearing it read may have a better understanding of how to go about setting up a PPB system to cover their own operations. The example of the PPBS model has been offered as a guide. Each manager should create his own plan to meet the needs of his special situation.

Remember, one of the keys to success in management is to be found in the ability to think creatively. As a manager or one in training for a position in management, you should be able to take an idea and see it quite clearly in all of its dimensions.

As an creative-thinking participant in this Institute On Library Management, you should be able to return to your libraries with certain basic concepts about PPB firmly established in your minds.

Harry Truman said it: "The buck stops here." It stops with you, the manager. You are the decision-maker, the creator, the businessman. **You** are that human resource which will make **your** program a success.

BIBLIOGRAPHY

1. Churchman, C. W. *Challenge to reason,* McGraw-Hill, 1968, p. 17

2. Eilon, S. *"What is a decision?",* Management Science,
    December 1969, p. B-172

3. Ibid., p. B-175

4. Ibid., p. B-177

5. Ibid., p. B-179

6. Ibid., p. B-179

7. Rockowner, I. *"Advice for Decision Makers",*
    Supervisory Management, p. 27

8. Ofstad, H. *An inquiry into the freedom of decision,*
    Allen and Unwin, 1961, p. ix

9. Suchochi, C. J. *"Don't let subordinates usurp your time",*
    Supervisory Management, May 1971, p. 39

10. Eilon, Ibid, p. B-174

11. International Encyclopedia of the Social Sciences, Vol. 1,
    p. 61-62

12. Bomberg, E., *Simplified PPBS for the libraries",*
    Dollar Decision Pre-conference Institute,
    American Library Association, 1971, p. 3

13. Schick, A. *"Systems politics and systems budgeting",*

Public Administration Review,
March/April 1969, p. 115

14. Grant, E. L. and Bell, L. F. *Basic accounting and cost accounting,*
McGraw-Hill, 1964, p. 466

15. Ibid., p. 466

16. Ibid., p. 466

17. Palmer, D. *Measuring library output,*
Institute on Program Planning and Budgeting Systems for Libraries,
Wayne State University, 1968, p. 109-110

18. Robinson, L. A. and Alexander, M. J. *"Are accountants adjusting to
change?",* Management Accounting, Nov. 1971, p. 11

19. Odom, G.T. *"Employee information system",* Management Accounting,
Nov. 1971, p. 20, 22

20. Combes, J. H. *Communication gaps: internal and external",*
Management Accounting, Nov. 1971, p. 27

21. Eggers, H. C. *"The evaluation of human assets",*
Management Accounting, Nov. 1971, p. 28

22. Moore, L. J. and Scott, D. F., Jr. *"Long-range planning and the
decentralized firm",* Management Accounting, Nov. 1971, p. 35

23. Sullivan, G.E. *"Modeling the university budget.",*
Management Accounting, Nov. 1971, p. 51

24. Management Accounting, Nov. 1971, p. 53

THE STATE OF MICHIGAN PROGRAM BUDGET EVALUATION SYSTEM AS APPLIED TO HIGHER EDUCATION

Philip Jager

Executive Office of the Governor
The State of Michigan

I am pleased to be a part of your conference today. Being the last individual on your program, I hope my remarks will reinforce rather than be redundant with what has been previously said.

Before I get too far into my subject, I should protect my flanks by mentioning that my wife is a professional librarian — retired as a homemaker for the time being — and has influenced my thinking as to what I should say to you today. So if you are bored or I miss my mark, it's her fault. Besides, as a speech topic, program budgeting is something like talking about a hippopotamus — pretty difficult to ignore its presence, but not too sexy.

With these excuses in mind, I'll try to stick to my topic which is the Program Budget System for Higher Education in the State of Michigan. With the help of a few illustrations, I'll try to leave you with the outline of the application of our system as we are now attempting to install it in Lansing.

But before I get into that, let me lay the ground work with some background of why we got to where we are. First of all, I would suggest very strongly that the concept of program budgeting is hardly new; however, its application has been a long time in coming.

Public budgeting in the executive branch of state, federal, and local governments has been evolving' in three stages since the early 1920's. Interestingly enough, the Executive Budget prior to that time was a virtual non-entity for federal, state and municipal governments. In those days budgets were not viewed as management tools of the executive branch of government. The first stage of executive budgeting development — which is still prevalent in some governmental jurisdictions — centered on accounting and expenditure control mechanisms. This development was an outgrowth and response to fraudulent expenditure practices of municipal governments which were criticized by reformists and muckrakers such as Upton Sinclair around the turn of the century. As a result of these exposures, budget processes were established whereby presidents, governors and mayors could be primarily concerned with the central accounting for the myriad of items necessary to the functioning of organizations under supervision. The focus tended to be of the "green eye shade" variety, a stereotype which has plagued many of us in this profession to this day.

The Roosevelt era produced the second stage of budgetary development. In that period, the Hoover Commission produced recommendation for "performance budgets", a term often interchanged nowadays with "program budgets." However, they are not the same thing. The performance budget was to stress the analysis of operational efficiency rather than just an accounting for the things and tools necessary to perform activities.

Budgetary analysis thus was still focusing on internal questions of efficiency involving the costs of those functions and activities being performed. It had not yet begun to look outward, as program budgeting is intended to do, to relate internal efficiency with outward effects. Did the efficient methods produce the results upon which they presumably justified themselves?

At any rate, the groundwork was starting to be laid for the shift in the mid-fifties which produced the program budget concept. As you know, this idea shifts the emphasis from the efficiency of work and service to be accomplished to the **planning for** and the **analysis of** the effective fulfillment of **objectives.** Activities, under the new concept, were no longer to be viewed as ends in themselves as was implicit in prior methods, but as intermediate steps toward some planned objective. The new concept forces a linkage for analysis of the product of the work being performed (outputs as we call it) to determine whether the expenditure makes any difference in attaining objectives.

The program concept, then, has been most recently established in the 1960's, but the seeds of this thinking clearly can be traced back to the 1920's, even though budgets at that time reflected the accounting-for-things approach. One student of government, Lent D. Upson, a Detroiter interested in government reform and active in the department of government at what is now Wayne State University, expressed criticism in the 1924 **Annals of the American Academy for Social and Political Science** that budgets contemporary to his time did not present a complete picture of what expenditures were intending to accomplish. He said that "the budget should be supplemented by an operations audit that will measure the effectiveness of expenditures as thoroughly as financial audits measure the legality of expenditures." Upson's words are still like a beacon to hone in on, and program budgeting efforts attempt to bring some of this earlier reformist thinking into a practical reality today.

In February, 1971, the Governor inaugurated a project within the Bureau of Programs and Budget to devote full time effort to the installation of a program budget system for the entire state. This has come to be known as the Program Budget Evaluation System or PBES for short. It is interesting that about the time the project was established, President Nixon coincidentally addressed Congress (March 25, 1971) on the need for government reorganization. His remarks are also, I think, an eloquent testimony for the program budgeting concept. He said that:

> "as our society has become more complex we often find ourselves using a variety of means to achieve a single set of goals ... We sometimes seem to have forgotten that government is not in business to deal with subjects on a chart, but to achieve real objectives for real human beings. These objectives will never be fully achieved unless we change our old ways of thinking ... We must rebuild the executive branch according to a new understanding of how government can best be organized to perform effectively."

Prior to 1971, the state was operating on what was viewed as a program budget, but the programs were clearly the servant of organizational units of the various state departments. Because organization predominated and influenced the way programs were presented and analyzed in the budget, programmatic analysis was conducted by looking down vertically into the organizational tumblers rather than horizontally through them. Another way of puting this is that similar programs were not classified according to their goals and objectives, but instead were prisoners of their organizational confines. This occured because no program structure existed which overrode the organizational considerations. Thus, the organizational cart was before the program horse. Criticism of the existing budgeting practices, in addition, surfaced other dissatisfactions as corollaries to this fundamental observation, namely:

a. the budget document did not contain adequate or appropriate information on which to formulate statewide decisions and policy determinations.

b. the document over-exposed numerical detail and provided only a minor amount of information on program goals, objectives and evaluation. In addition, these terms were loosely defined and unevenly applied.

c. the budget process gave little emphasis to planning beyond the fiscal period of the budget being presented.

d. there was not sufficient emphasis devoted to measuring outputs which are direct services to the public and whether the services were achieving their intended purposes.

The separate project unit was set up to correct these problems. Its objective was to classify all the state's governmental activities into a structure which focused on programs regardless of their organizational relationship. The project office could work on a rigid and orderly timetable to complete this task, free from the day to day workload pressures which precluded the Budget Division from accomplishing this mission.

The Project Office's charge was to quarterback the conversion of the existing budget to the program format for fiscal 1973-74. It was given a specific timetable for a two year period in which specific events had to occur. Upon completion of the preliminary work in developing the structure and mechanics of the system, the Project Office will be dissolved. The system will be implemented by the Budget Division beginning with the 1973-74 request period. The timetable is approximately on schedule as it was originally envisioned, and we are now at the point where the overall state program structure has been developed, and information is being tailored to its design.

Let me now give you the framework for the application of the system in general and how it affects higher education in particular. In establishing the budget structure and making all activities get into it, eight major programs were established as "givens". A very good and critical student of the pragmatics of the budget process, Professor Aaron Wildavsky, has made the point that "Programs are not made in heaven, there is nothing out there that is just waiting to be found. Programs are not natural to the world; they must be imposed on it by men. No one can give instructions for making up programs. There are as many ways to conceive of programs as there are of organizing activity."

In passing I might remark that this first step caused much dismay and argument in agencies over whether these major programs were appropriate and whether there shouldn't be six, or ten or whatever. Because the whole process would be doomed before it started if the academics of this debate got out of control, all other options were foreclosed. The eight major programs which were utilized to classify governmental activities are cited in **Visual 1.**

Major programs were to be broken down into three strata: program categories, program subcategories, and program elements. For approximately six months after the inception of the project, project personnel spent their time in assisting agencies and institutions in developing the taxonomy of the structure.

The eight major programs are value-laden with stated broad goals which have no time constraints. **(See Visual 2).** As movement is made down the structure hierarchy to the level of the program category, the goals become slightly more specific, but are still broad and, in effect, constitute plateaus to strive for. The major program and program category levels serve as the general aggregators or the overall collection points for costs and points to reach toward in terms of attainment. Beyond that, they don't tell you too much by way of specifics.

The program subcategories become the focal point of the structure. **(See Visual 3).** It is at this level that objectives are specified and what we call "impact indicators" are introduced. The logic of the structure requires an expression of objectives in terms of effects upon individuals, institutions, and the environ-

VISUAL 1

THE MICHIGAN PROGRAM PLAN
EIGHT MAJOR PROGRAMS

1. Protection of Persons & Property
2. Health — Physical and Mental well-being
3. Intellectual Development and Education
4. Social Development
5. Economic Development
6. Transportation and Communication
7. Recreation and Cultural Enrichment
8. Direction and Support

VISUAL 2

MICHIGAN PROGRAM PLAN STRUCTURE

MAJOR PROGRAM
1. Goals-Unconstrained by time
2.
3.
4.
5.
6.
7.
8.

PROGRAM CATEGORIES
1. Subgoals-Unconstrained by time
2.
3.

PROGRAM SUBCATEGORIES
1. Objective-Impacts
2.
3.

PROGRAM ELEMENTS
1. Outputs & Need/Demand
2.
3.

VISUAL 3

DEFINITIONS

OBJECTIVE — A desired quantitiable change in a condition within a specific time frame, which will contribute toward the attainment of the goals expressed in the Michigan Program Plan.

IMPACT
INDICATOR — A quantitative expression of the subcategory objective statement; a measure which describes the effect programs have upon individuals, the environment, or other institutions.

OUTPUT
MEASURE — Quantitiable units produced as a result of activities carried out at the element level.

NEED —
DEMAND
ESTIMATOR — A quantitative measure of the magnitude of a problem which determines the required size of an element's output production in response to that problem.

ment, not in terms of how much work is being performed. Objective achievement, therefore, must be stated in terms of what the organization accomplishes in the world external to it rather than in the terms of the level of its own activity.

The impact indicator is a statistical measuring device, which is used to ascertain whether the outputs of the next level of the structure, the program element, are having any effect on the objective expressed at the subcategory level. The element level of the structure is clearly the real world where the action is; it accounts for departmental activities and the products of the work being performed. The "crunch point" in the structure is the relationship of these work products (or outputs) to the subcategory level's objective attainment as expressed in the impact measure. If, over time, the outputs do not benefit the objectives as reflected in impact indicators, this will suggest the necessity to modify or eliminate the element composition, scale down or restate the objectives, or perhaps add elements which, through analysis, show the possibility of achieving the impacts.

Another statistic used at the element level in addition to the output measure is the need-demand estimator. This information shows the magnitude of a problem which determinates the required size of an element's output production in response to that problem. One example of need-demand would be the number of students applying for admission to a particular program or institution. Projections for impacts, outputs, and need-demand are made over a five-year time frame.

In general, the design objective for the structure is to develop and install a politically responsive, research oriented and information-sensitive decision making system. Again the primary intent of the system which must be stressed is the structural relationship of outputs to impact achievement.

The National Center for Higher Education Management Systems of the Western Interstate Commission on Higher Education recently emphasized this point in one of their bulletins. Imagine, they said,

> "a housewife entering an appliance store to buy a washing machine. The salesman is charming and helpful. 'Here's one,' he says, 'its price is $239.50.' 'Does it get clothes clean?' she asks. 'Oh, we don't know that,' the salesman replies. 'All we know is how much it costs.' Silly scenario, indeed. Yet this exchange, with a different cast, different script, and different scenery takes place daily in the environment of higher education decision-making. ... What higher education has done in the past and continues to do in the present is to center its attention on the historical costs of higher education as the primary basis for making decisions. ... However, cost information alone doesn't tell anything about the

outcomes and benefits attained by implementation of a particular decision."

Hopefully, this will give you some background and a general idea of what we are trying to do within the concept of the structure. It's really a simple idea that is difficult to execute. Now let's turn to its applications in higher education.

The major program "intellectual development and education," which we call Program III, has two program categories, education for youth and education for adults. These categories in turn, break down into many specific subcategory objectives which in turn are the basis for the output production at the element level. In Program III we find elements relating to the Mental Health Department services to retarded children as well as activities of local school boards, the Department of Education and higher education institutions. These elements are keyed to specific subcategory objectives.

Higher education branches off the category "education for adults." As you can determine by referring to **Visuals 4 and 5,** the structure contains a maximum of 19 subcategories and 108 elements for the higher education portion. Since programs at each institution vary in scope and complexity, it is highly unlikely that these maximum numbers would be used by any one institution.

A basic premise underlying the higher education portion of the structure is that education has a fundamental relationship to manpower objectives which can be expressed at the subcategory levels in the form of subject fields. The elements related to these subcategories are classified by level of instruction such as lower division instruction and so forth. The outputs at this level, defined as credit hours, degrees, certificates and the like, will be related to the achievement of manpower objectives for the subject fields. **(See Visual 6).**

This structure was a difficult one to develop and went through many re-drafts as the result of discussions and/or disputes with institutions. It was finally decided to model the subcategories of the structure on work being done at the federal level by the National Center for Higher Education Management Systems at the Western Interstate Commission on Higher Education (WICHE). The instructional subcategories have been crossreferenced to taxonomies developed by the United States Department of Health, Education and Welfare for the Higher Education General Information Survey (HEGIS). The use of this taxonomy and crosswalk provides reasonably uniform guidance for reporting and relating activities to the subcategories and elements.

You can also see by referring to exhibits that your field of interest, libraries, is considered as an element of the academic support subcategory. Institutional library services as well as that portion of library services related to higher education, as provided

VISUAL 4

THE PROGRAM STRUCTURE FOR HIGHER EDUCATION

SUBCATEGORY

ELEMENT

Instruction: (12 SUBCATEGORIES BY SELECTED HEGIS GROUPING)

(INSTRUCTION ELEMENTS REPLICATED FOR EACH SUBCATEGROY AS APPROPRIATE)

Agricultural & Natural Resource Instruction
- Lower Division – General Academic
- Upper Division – GeneralAcademic
- Occupational & Vocational
- Masters
- Doctors and Intermediate
- First Professional

Arts Humanities and Letters

Biological Sciences

Business Management and Commerce

Computers and Information Science

Education

Engineering, Arch and Rel Tech Fields

Health Science Professions

Law

Physical Science and Math

Social Sciences, Human Service, and Public Affairs

Other

VISUAL 5

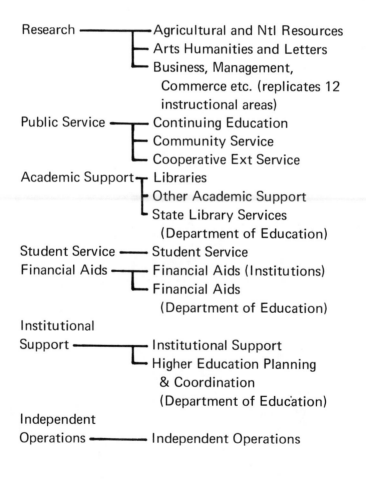

**THE PROGRAM STRUCTURE
FOR HIGHER EDUCATION**

SUBCATEGORY   ELEMENT

Research ———————— Agricultural and Ntl Resources
          Arts Humanities and Letters
          Business, Management,
           Commerce etc. (replicates 12
           instructional areas)
Public Service ————— Continuing Education
          Community Service
          Cooperative Ext Service
Academic Support ——— Libraries
          Other Academic Support
          State Library Services
           (Department of Education)
Student Service ————— Student Service
Financial Aids ————— Financial Aids (Institutions)
          Financial Aids
           (Department of Education)
Institutional
Support ———————— Institutional Support
          Higher Education Planning
           & Coordination
           (Department of Education)
Independent
Operations ———————— Independent Operations

VISUAL 6

SUBCATEGORY EXTRACT OF PROGRAM III – INTELLECTUAL DEVELOPMENT & EDUCATION

SUBCATEGORY: Agricultural and Natural Resources Instruction

IMPACT
INDICATORS: Percent and number of students finding career placement within 6 months of graduation

Percent and number of students finding educationally related placement within 6 months

Mean entry level salary of graduates

ELEMENT: Lower Division General Academic Instruction — Upper Division General Academic Instruction

OUTPUT
MEASUREMENTS: Credit Hours — Credit hours
Certificates
Associate degrees — Bachelors degrees

RESOURCE
REQUIREMENTS: Financial in dollars by source; manpower in manyears by labor classification, e.g., faculty, service, professional administrative.

by the Department of Education's State Library, show up here. The State Library, by the way, is included not only as an element of this major program, but within two others as well. This illustrates again our desire to show programmatic relationship of organizational production to specific objectives as they appear within major programs.

Each institution of higher education is now classifying its entire operations into this portion of the major program III hierarchy. The structure is the basis for the Institution Program Plan. This IPP, as we call it, contains three basic types of information. These basic information blocks are: 1) the program statement which details the specific impact indicators for each subcategory and the element output and need/demand estimators; 2) the financial statement giving the specific expenditure information for each element; and 3) the manpower classification for each element. **(See Visual 7).** This information also is to be projected for five years.

By aggregating each institution's portion of the elements and subcategories, we can see, for example, what is being done to meet statewide objectives of educating for the health professions. We will be able to analyze this information shown in elements for the subcategory by level of instruction and type of degree, and relate this production to the impact indicators and to the need/demand statistics. This process can be repeated for each subcategory within the structure by subcategory field.

Practically all of the work to date in launching the system has been involved with getting the structure and its financial manpower, and output-impact statistic into place.

I should now give you an idea of what is involved in the decision cycle for PBES. The structure is the necessary first part of a process which has four important events. **(Visual 8).**

All Institutional Program Plans based on this structure become a part of the whole, or what is known as the Michigan Program Plan. This is simply the summation of all elements and subcategories of each major program to the category and major program levels.

This accomplishes the conversion to the Michigan Program Plan. The program budget cycle then starts in the spring with the Governor's issuance of Program Policy Guidelines. These guidelines are a statement of issue as related to structure which the Governor and his staff see as needing resolution. These issues can open up the entire structure and its objectives for review or, more likely, can key on selected items that have political relevancy. Agencies respond to these guidelines as appropriate, indicating changes in their program plans through what is called the program revision request. This document outlines the steps and alternatives necessary to accomplish new or modified output changes at the element level in order to resolve the issues cited

VISUAL 7

IPP CONTENTS

PROGRAM STATEMENT
   SUBCATEGORY IMPACT INDICATORS
   ELEMENT OUTPUT MEASURES
   ELEMENT NEED/DEMAND ESTIMATORS

FINANCIAL STATEMENT
   SUBCATEGORY SUMMARY
   ELEMENT DETAILED
   ELEMENT SUMMARY

MANPOWER STATEMENT
   ELEMENT

VISUAL 8

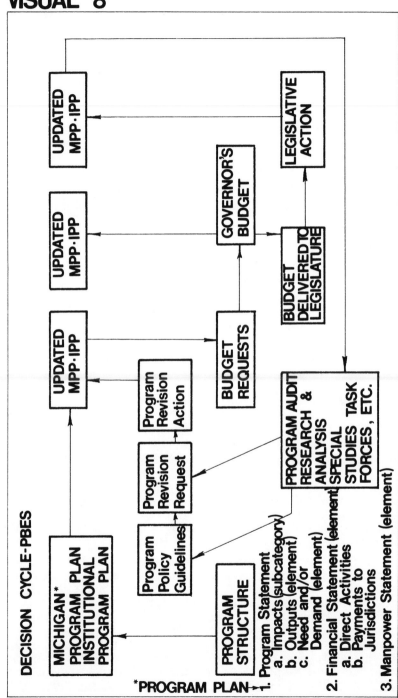

DECISION CYCLE-PBES

MICHIGAN* PROGRAM PLAN INSTITUTIONAL PROGRAM PLAN

Program Policy Guidelines

Program Revision Request

Program Revision Action

UPDATED MPP·IPP

UPDATED MPP·IPP

UPDATED MPP·IPP

BUDGET REQUESTS

GOVERNOR'S BUDGET

BUDGET DELIVERED TO LEGISLATURE

LEGISLATIVE ACTION

PROGRAM STRUCTURE

PROGRAM AUDIT RESEARCH & ANALYSIS SPECIAL STUDIES TASK FORCES, ETC.

*PROGRAM PLAN→ 1. Program Statement (subcategory)
a. Impacts (subcategory)
b. Outputs (element)
c. Need and/or Demand (element)
2. Financial Statement (element)
a. Direct Activities
b. Payments to Jurisdictions
3. Manpower Statement (element)

in the guidelines. Program hearings related to these requests will be organized around program structure subcategories. In attendance will be program managers of the elements related to the subcategories. In most instances they will be from different departments.

The new system advances the budget timeable so that issues are addressed during the spring and summer. Program revision actions based on the hearings will be relayed back to agencies and institutions in late summer so they will be in a position to incorporate approved program changes in their budget requests.

Research and special studies relating outputs to impacts will heavily influence both the content of the program policy guidelines and the program revision requests. Requests which are not responsive to the guidelines or do not address the requirements for analysis of program alternatives are not likely to receive serious consideration as part of budget office review or be incorporated into the updated Michigan program plan as an approved program revision action.

In sum, the program structure transcends organization and puts information in a format which encourages some of the right questions to be asked. What we consider the "right" questions in the impact oriented structure are usually those which impose an implicit threat to traditional assumptions. The structure and its application do not permit the luxury of casual assumptions that certain effects will occur (impacts) if certain activities (outputs) are carried out. It has become evident with the development of PBES, that there is a paucity of information for testing the validity of existing doctrine, a function of analysis. But the identification of the absence of data is a necessary step to develop information requirements for a reporting system that will satisfy the needs for program management and analysis.

Establishing this system is not a bed of roses. The confrontation of the old budgeting methods with the new systems budgeting will result in recurring conflict until program budgeting demonstrates its superiority over the old methods where "things" rather than "effects" were the primary concern of budgeteers. This will continue for some time since the skeptics of the new system have had nearly forty to fifty years to become ensconced in their traditional ways of doing things.

I know that this process has caused some understandable paranoia on the part of many. This is because the method requires individuals involved in planning and budgeting to develop attitudes different from those under conventional budgeting patterns. These people now have to view their roles in a future time perspective rather than in a present time perspective. The combination of this factor with the need to still satisfy fiduciary and other reporting responsibilities — since the program budget is not intended, for example, as an internal institutional accounting statement — will make many feel like they're caught between bases.

We have many people who react like the director of a local drug program. Under pressure by the Country Board of Commissioners to show results for his program, he stated, as quoted in the **Detroit News:**

> "People who are asking how effective the centers are certainly deserve a straight answer, but I can truthfully say I don't know. If we stop to evaluate, we stop functioning, it's that simple. It's always a struggle. We agree (the officials) should know how many people we are serving and whether the money they are spending is having any effect... In our type of program, we emphasize people, and sort of deemphasize categorization and paperwork. So in a sense we work against establishing our legitimacy."

We recognize these as natural inclinations, but they have been the prevailing attitude for too long. We are in effect saying, let's make your unstated program assumptions naked in the structure to see if they really stand up. We believe sound public policy forces us to use a vehicle in which presumed program legitimacy and claims of effectiveness can be tested.

In any system, there is always the danger that process will smother substance. We are working very hard to not smother programs in pseudo-analysis, but we do insist that effectiveness of programs continues to be challenged based on achievement of objectives. While these kinds of questions have been asked all along, we believe the PBE System will now give us a disciplined approach by which budgeting becomes more effective and an improved standard which is to be adhered to by all.

PPBS
A BIBLIOGRAPHIC SURVEY

By

MARGARET EIDE
Head, Social Sciences Division
Eastern Michigan University

INTRODUCTION

As the four conference speakers emphasized, PPBS is not new. Even the acronym has been in use for close to a decade, and the concept was in use by General Motors as early as 1924. Since each extension of application has generated new interest and, of course, additional literature, the amount of printed material currently available concerning PPBS is overwhelming. The titles cited on the following pages do not represent an exhaustive listing but rather a wide selection designed to provide both general background and history and specifically-oriented information for those concerned with state and local government, higher education and libraries.

GENERAL BACKGROUND AND HISTORY

Monographs

Alfandary-Alexander, Mark, Comp.
Analysis for planning, programming, budgeting: second cost-effectiveness symposium. Sponsored by Washington Operations Research Council, Potomac, Md., 1968. 174 p.

American Enterprise Institute for Public Policy Research.
Congress and the federal budget,
Washington, D.C., AEIPPR, 1965. 209 p.

American Society of Planning Officials.
Planning-programming-budgeting systems, papers presented at PPBS short course held at 1969 ASPO National Planning Conference, ed. by Virginia Curtis, Chicago, ASPO, 1969. 54 p.

Anshen, Melvin.
The program budget in operation. Santa Monica,
Rand Corp., 1965. 20 p.

Archibald, K. A.
PPB systems and program evaluation. Santa Monica,
Rand Corp., 1970. 9 p.

Art, Robert J.
The TFX decision: McNamara and the military.
Boston, Little, Brown, 1968.

Bell, Chauncey F.
Cost-effective analysis as a management tool.
Santa Monica, Rand Corp., 1964. 52 p.

Black, Guy.
The application of systems analysis to government operations.
New York, Praeger, 1968.

Buchanan, James M.
Cost and choice: an inquiry in economic theory.
Chicago, Markham, 1969.

Burkhead, Jesse.
Government budgeting. New York, Wiley, 1966. 498 p.

Chackerian, Richard.
Selected bibliography on public budgeting. Seattle, University of Washington, Bureau of Governmental and Service, 1968. 6 p.

Chartrand, Robert L., editor.
Information support, program budgeting and the Congress.
New York, Spartan, 1968. 231 p.

Chase, Samuel B., editor.
Problems in public expenditure analysis. Washington, D. C.
Brookings Institution, 1966.

Christenson, Charles.
Program budgeting. Washington, D. C.,
Management Analysis Center, Inc., 1968.

Cleland, David I. and William R. King, editors.
Systems, organizations, analysis, management: a book of readings. New York, McGraw-Hill, 1969.

Colm, Gerhard.
Program planning for national goals. Washington, National
Planning Association, 1968.
Committee for Economic Development. Research and Policy Com.
Budgeting for national objectives: executive and Congressional
roles in program planning and performance.
New York, Committee for Economic Development, 1966. 65 p.
Cost-effectiveness Symposium, 2d, 1967.
Analysis for planning programming budgeting. Potomac,
Maryland, Washington Operations Research Council, 1968. 174 p.
Council of Planning Librarians.
Planning-programming-budgeting systems, by Dean Tudor,
Monticello, Illinois, 1970. Exchange bibliography 121. 19 p.
Council of Planning Librarians.
Planning, programming, budgeting systems (A Supplement to
Exchange Bibliography No. 121 of March 1970), by Dean Tudor.
Monticello, Illinois, 1971. Exchange bibliography 183. 5 p.
Crowe, Eugene B. and Delmas D. Ray.
"Planning-Programming-Budgeting Systems" **Economic Leaflets,**
vol. 28, no. 5, 6, 7, May-July 1969. 12 p.
Detroit Public Library. Municipal Reference Library.
Programming, planning, budgeting systems; a selected list of
recent references. **MRL Bulletin,** January, 1969. 6 p.
Doh, Joon Chien.
The planning-programming-budgeting systems in three federal
agencies. New York, Praeger, 1971. 192 p.
Donvito, P. A.
Annotated bibliography on systems cost analysis.
Santa Monica, Rand Corp., 1967. 85 p.
Dorfman, Robert.
Measuring benefits of government investments.
New York, McGraw-Hill, 1965.
Dror, Yehezkel.
Public policymaking reexamined. San Francisco,
Chandler Pub. Co., 1968.
Edwards, Edgar O., editor.
The nation's economic objectives. Chicago, University
of Chicago Press, 1964.
Else, Peter.
Public expenditure, parliament and PPB. London, Political and
Economic Planning, November 1970. 92 p.
English, J. M. and R. H. Haase.
Economic selection of alternative risk investments.
Santa Monica, Rand Corp., 1964, 16 p.
Enke, Stephen, editor.
Defence management. Englewood Cliffs, New Jersey,
Prentice-Hall, 1967.
Fisher, G. H.
The role of cost-utility analysis in program budgeting.
Santa Monica, Rand Corp., 1964. 46 p.

Fisher, G. H.
What is resource analysis? Santa Monica, Rand Corp., 1963.
Fisher, G. H.
The world of program budgeting. Santa Monica,
Rand Corp., 1966. 30 p.
Fox, Thomas G.
An introduction to planning-programming-budgeting systems
(PPBS). University Park, Pennsylvania, Pennsylvania State
University Institute for Research on Human Resources,
Feb. 28, 1967. 14 p.
Goldman, Thomas A., editor.
Cost-effectiveness analysis: new approaches in decision-making.
New York, Praeger, 1966.
Grosse, Robert N.
An introduction to cost-effectiveness analysis. McLean,
Virginia, Research Analysis Corp., 1965.
Grosse, Robert N.
Principles of cost-effectiveness analysis, Washington, D. C.
Industrial College of the Armed Forces, 1965.
Haldi, John.
Criteria for definition of program categories and program ele-
ments. Remarks before the U. S. Naval Post Graduate School,
Defense Management Systems Course, Monterey, California, 1965.
Washington, D. C., U. S. Bureau of the Budget, 1966.
Haldi, John.
Issues of analysis in cost-effectiveness studies for civilian agen-
cies of the federal government. Paper presented at the Institute
of Management Sciences, September 7, 1966, Philadelphia, Penn-
sylvania. Washington, D. C., U. S. Bureau of the Budget, 1966.
Haldi, John.
A report on planning-programming-budgeting. Washington, D.C.,
U. S. Bureau of the Budget, 1966.
Haveman, Robert H. and Julius Margolis, editors.
Public expenditures and policy analysis.
Chicago, Markham Pub. Co., 1970, 596 p.
Haveman, Robert H.
Unemployment, idle capacity, and the evaluation of public ex-
penditure: National and regional analyses. Baltimore,
John Hopkins Press 1968. 150 p.
Hawaii. Legislature. Office of the Legislative Auditor.
PPBS bibliography. Rev. June 1, 1970. Honolulu, 1970.
Hawaii. State Library.
PPB bibliography. TAC publication no. 70-2325. Honolulu,
Office of Library Service, 1971. 53 p.
Hetrick, Marjory H.
Planning-programming budgeting systems: selected bibliography
of recent articles and monographs available in the Pennsylvania
State Library. Harrisburg, Pennsylvania State Library,
General Library Bureau, 1969. 4 p.

Hinrichs, Harley H. and Graeme M. Taylor.
Program budgeting and benefit-cost analysis: cases, text and readings. Pacific Palisades, California, Goodyear, 1969. 420 p.

Hirsch, Werner Z.
Integrating view of Federal program budgeting. Santa Monica, Rand Corp., 1966. 27 p.

Hirsch, Werner Z.
Program budget for natural resources activities. Santa Monica, Rand Corp., 1965. 38 p.

Hirsch, Werner Z. and Sidney Sonenblum.
Selecting regional information for government planning and decision-making. New York, Praeger, 1970.

Hitch, Charles J.
Decision-making for defense. Berkeley and Los Angeles, University of California Press, 1965.

Hitch, Charles J. and Ronald N. McKean
The economics of defense in the nuclear age.
New York, Atheneum, 1965.

Hovey, Harold A.
The planning-programming- budgeting approach to government decision making. New York, Praeger, 1968. 264 p.

Howell, David.
Programme budgeting and its implications for public accountability and government structure in the United Kingdom. Paper presented at a seminar at the Institute of Government and Public Affairs, University of California, May 14, 1969. Los Angeles, Institute of Government and Public Affairs,
University of California, 1969.

Jones, Reginald L. and H. George Trentin.
Budgeting: Key to planning and control, practical guidelines for managers. New York, American Management Association, Inc., 1971. 308 p.

Kahn, Herman and Irwin Mann.
Techniques of systems analysis. Santa Monica, Rand Corp., 1957.

Lecht, Leonard A.
Goals, priorities and dollars - the next decade.
New York, Free Press, 1966.

Lehan, Edward A.
Program budgeting. University of Connecticut, Institute of Public Services, 1969. 24 p.

Leontief, Wassily.
Input-output of economics. New York, Oxford University Press, 1966.

Levin, Melvin R.
Community and regional planning: issues in public policy. New York, Praeger, 1969. 305 p.

Lyden, Fremont J. and Ernest G. Miller, editors.
Planning, programming, budgeting: a systems approach to management. Chicago, Markham Pub. Co., 1967. 443 p.

McCullough, J. D.
Cost analysis for planning-programming-budgeting: cost-benefit studies. Santa Monica, Rand Corp., 1966. 64 p.

McCullough, J. D.
Cost effectiveness: estimating systems costs. Santa Monica, Rand Corp., 1965. 26 p.

McKean, Roland N.
Efficiency in government through systems analysis, with emphasis on water resources development. New York, Wiley, 1958.

McKean, Roland N.
Efficiency in government through systems analysis. New York, Wiley, 1966. 336 p.

McKean, Roland N.
Problems, limitations and risks of the program budget. Santa Monica, Rand Corp., 1965. 23 p.

Marglin, Stephen A.
Public investment criteria; benefit-cost analysis for planned economic growth. Cambridge, Massachusetts Institute of Technology Press, 1966.

Miller, Ernest Charles.
Objectives and standards: an approach to planning and control. New York, American Management Association, 1966. Research study 74.

Miller, Ernest Charles.
Objectives and standards of performance in financial management. New York, American Management Association, 1968. Research study 87.

Miller, Ernest Charles.
Objectives and standards of performance in production management. New York, American Management Association, 1967. Research study 84.

Mitchell, Edward E. Analysis — the keystone to a planning-programming-budgeting system. Stanford Research Institute, April 1967. 20 p.

Moak, Lennox and Kathryn W. Killian.
A manual of techniques for the preparation, consideration, adoption, and administration of operating budgets. New York, Municipal Finance Officers Association, 1954.

Morse, Philip M., editor.
Operations research for public systems. Cambridge, Massachusetts Institute of Technology Press, 1967.

Mosher, Frederick C.
Program budgeting: theory and practice, with particular reference to the U. S. Dept. of the Army. New York, Public Administration Service. 1954. 258 p.

Mosher, Frederick C. and John E. Harr.
Programming systems and foreign affairs leadership; an attempted innovation. New York, Oxford University Press, 1970, 261 p.

Municipal Finance Officers Association of the United States
and Canada.
Economy, effectiveness, and efficiency in budgeting,
by Monty C. Lish and Lloyd F. Hara. Chicago, 1970.
National Industrial Conference Board.
The federal budget: its impact on the economy.
New York, Tax Foundation, 1967.
Newman, William H., Charles E. Summer,
and E. Kirby Warren, editors.
The process of management; concepts, behaviour, and practice.
2nd ed. Englewood Cliffs, New Jersey, Prentice-Hall, 1967.
Novick, David.
Efficiency and economy in government through new budgeting
and accounting procedures. Santa Monica, Rand Corp. 1954. 122 p.
Novick, David.
Program analysis revisited. Santa Monica, Rand Corp., 1971. 11 p.
Novick, David.
Program budgeting; long-range planning in the Department of
Defense. Santa Monica, Rand Corp., 1962. 16 p.
Novick, David, editor.
Program budgeting, program analysis and the federal budget.
Cambridge, Massachusetts, Harvard University Press, 1965.
382 p. (The "classic" on PPB).
Novick, David, editor.
Program budgeting, program analysis and the federal budget.
Bureau of the Budget. 1965. 236 p. (An abridgment of the
Harward University Press Publication. Each chapter also
appeared as a Rand Corporation Memorandum).
Novick, David, editor.
Program budgeting. 2nd edition. Cambridge, Massachusetts,
Harward University, 1967.
Novick, David.
Resource analysis and long-range planning.
Santa Monica, Rand Corp., 1963. 22 p.
Novick, David.
Which program do we mean in "Program Bdugeting"?
Santa Monica, Rand Corp., 1952, 31 p.
Ontario. Treasury Board.
Effective management through P.P.B.S. Toronto, 1969. 68 p.
Ontario. Treasury Board.
Program budgeting — a discussion paper for the Continuing
Committee on Fiscal and Economic Matters, May 1968. 14 p.
Operations Research Industries Ltd.
The Department of Highways, Ontario; planning-programming-
budgeting system. Ottawa, August 1969. 1. V.
(PPBS Management Study — Final Report).
Optner, Stanford L.
Systems analysis for business and industrial problem solving.
Englewood Cliffs. New Jersey, Prentice-Hall, 1965. 116 p.

Orkand, Donald S.
An overview of planning, programming and management. Silver Spring, Maryland, Operations Research, Inc., 1967. 31 p.

Ott, David J. and Attiat F. Ott.
Federal budget policy. Washington, D. C., Brookings Institution, 1965.

Quade, E. S., editor.
Analysis for military decisions. Chicago, Rand McNally, 1967.

Quade, E. S.
Some problems associated with systems analysis. Santa Monica, Rand Corp., 1966. 21 p.

Quade, E. S. and W. I. Boucher.
Systems analysis and policy planning: application in defense. New York, American Elsevier Pub. Co., 1968.

Quade, E. S.
Systems analysis techniques for planning-programming-budgeting, Santa Monica, Rand Corp., 1966. 31 p.

Rowen, Henry S.
Statement before the Special Subcommittee on Scientific Manpower Utilization of the Senate Labor and Public Welfare Committee. Washington, D. C., U. S. Bureau of the Budget, 1966.

Samuelson, Paul A.
Economics: an introductory analysis. New York, McGraw-Hill, 1964.

Schick, Allen.
Some problems of the multipurpose budget system. Washington, D. C., U. S. Bureau of the Budget, Program Evaluation Staff, 1966.

Schlesinger, James R.
Systems analysis and the political process. Santa Monica, Rand Corp., 1967. 31 p.

Schultze, C. L.
The politics and economics of public spending. Washington, D. C., Brookings Institution, 1968. 143 p.

Schwartz, Edward E., editor.
Planning, programming, budgeting systems and social welfare. Chicago, University of Chicago, School of Social Service Administration, 1970. 58 p.

Sewell, A. R. D., et al.
Guide to benefit-cost analysis. Ottawa, Canada, Queen's Printer, 1965. 49 p.

Sharkansky, Ira, editor.
Policy analysis in political science. Chicago, Markham Pub. Co., 1970.

Smithies, Arthur.
A conceptual framework for the program budget. Santa Monica, Rand Corp., 1964. 48 p.

Smithies, Arthur.
  Government decision-making and the theory of choice.
  Santa Monica, Rand Corp., 1964. 11 p.
Stanford Research Institute.
  Programming — a context for decision making in government
  and industry. Menlo Park, California, 1965.
Tar, N. W.
  Benefit-cost analysis review. Toronto, Dept. of Economics and
  Development, Economic Analysis Branch, 1966. 27 p.
Tax Foundation.
  Planning-programming-budgeting systems and cost-benefit
  analysis in government. New York, 1967.
  Research bibliography, no. 26. 4 p.
Terhune, George A.
  Performance and program budgeting practices in the United
  States and Canada. Chicago, Municipal Finance Officers
  Association of the United States and Canada, 1966.
Tolmachev, Mirjana.
  Planning-programming-budgeting systems: selected bibliography
  of recent articles and monographs available in the Pennsylvania
  State Library. 2nd edition. Harrisburg, Pennsylvania State
  Library, General Library Bureau, 1970. 5 p.
United Nations. Dept. of Economic and Social Affairs.
  A manual for programme and performance budgeting.
  New York, 1965. 103 p.
U. S. Bureau of the Budget.
  Bureau of the budget and program evaluation.
  Washington, D. C., 1966. 13 p.
U. S. Bureau of the Budget.
  Discount rates and procedures to be used in evaluating deferred
  costs and benefits. Washington, D. C., 1969.
  Circular no. A-94. 1969.
U. S. Bureau of the Budget.
  Evaluation, review, and coordination of federal assistance
  programs and projects. Washington, D. C., 1969.
  Circular no. A-95, 1969.
U. S. Bureau of the Budget.
  The federal planning-programming-budgeting system, remarks
  by Frank W. Krause, Washington, D. C., February 4, 1966. 12 p.
U. S. Bureau of the Budget.
  "Improving decision making in government." Address delivered
  by Henry S. Rowen at a meeting of the Budget Bureau's Summer
  Seminar on Systems Analysis and Program Evaluation,
  August 19, 1965.
U. S. Bureau of the Budget.
  Memorandum on planning-programming-budgeting.
  Washington D. C., 1965. Bulletin no. 66-3, October 12, 1965. 15 p.
U. S. Bureau of the Budget.

Planning-programming-budgeting (PPB).
Washington, D. C., 1967. Bulletin no. 68-2, July 18, 1967. 14 p.
U. S. Bureau of the Budget.
Planning-programming-budgeting (PPB) system.
Washington D. C., 1968. Bulletin no. 68-9, April 12, 1968,
and supplement no. 1, July 17, 1969.
U. S. Bureau of the Budget.
Preparation and submission of annual budget estimates.
Washington, D. C., 1970. Circular no. A-11, rev., June 15, 1970.
U. S. Bureau of the Budget. Library.
Program analysis techniques; a selected bibliography. Rev.
Washington D. C., 1966. 33 p. Supplements, 1967, 40 p.
and 1969, 27 p.
U. S. Civil Service Commission.
Teaching cases in planning, programming, budgeting.
Washington, D. C., Bureau of Training, Financial Management
and PPB Training Center, U. S. Civil Service Commission, 1969.
U. S. Civil Service Commission. Bureau of Training.
A follow-up study of the three-week residential seminar in PPBS.
Washington, D. C., 1968. 98 p.
U. S. Comptroller General.
Survey of progress in implementing the planning-programming-
budgeting system in executive agencies. Washington, D. C.,
General Accounting Office, July 1969. 103 p.
U. S. Congress. House of Representatives.
Message from the President of the United States transmitting
reorganization plan no. 2 of 1970, 91st Cong., 2nd session, March
12, 1970. Washington D. C., Government Printing Office, 1970.
Document no. 91-275.
U. S. Congress. House of Representatives. Committee on Science
and Astronautics.
A technology assessment system for the executive branch
(report prepared by National Academy of Public Administration
Ad Hoc Panel on Technology Assessment).
Washington, D. C., Government Printing Office, 1970.
U. S. Congress. House of Representatives. Subcommittee
on Government Operations.
Effective and efficient use of computers in Congress, Hearings,
91st Congress, 1st session, April 23, 1969. Washington D. C.,
Government Printing Office, 1969.
U. S. Congress. Joint Economic Committee. Subcommittee
on Economic Statistics.
The Federal budget as an economic document, 88th Congress,
1st session, report no. 396. Washington, D. C.,
Government Printing Office, 1963.
U. S. Congress. Joint Economic Committee. Subcommittee
on Economy in Government.
Analysis and evaluation of public expenditures: the PPB system,

a compendium of papers, 91st Congress, 1st session, Washington, D. C., Government Printing Office, 1969. Contests: Volume 1: Part I. The appropriate functions of government in an enterprise system. Part. II. Institutional factors affecting efficient public expenditure policy. Part III. Some problems of analysis in evaluating public expenditure alternatives. Volume 2: Part IV. The current status of the planning-programming-budgeting system. Volume 3: Part V. The performance of program budgeting and analysis in the federal government. Part. VI: Analysis and evaluation in major policy areas: unresolved issues and next steps. (Material provided by 57 invited experts; this publication contains a wealth of information).

U. S. Congress. Joint Economic Committee. Subcommittee on Economy in Government.
Changing national priorities, part 1 and 2. Hearings. 91st Congress, 2nd session, June, 1970, Washington D. C., Government Printing Office, 1970.

U. S. Congress. Joint Economic Committee. Subcommittee on Economy in Government.
Economic analysis and the efficiency of government. Report, together with supplementary views of Senator Charles H. Percy. 91st Congress, 2nd Session. Washington, U. S. Government Printing Office, February 9, 1970. (Based on hearings held by the subcommittee as a followup to its 3-volume study, published in 1969.)

U. S. Congress. Joint Economic Committee. Subcommittee on Economy in Government.
Economic analysis and the efficiency of government, part. 3. Hearings, 91st Congress, 1st Session. September 30, 1969. Washington D. C., Government Printing Office, 1970, p. 694-706, 758-788.

U. S. Congress. Joint Economic Committee. Subcommittee on Economy in Government.
Economic analysis of public investment decisions: interest rate policy and discounting analysis, a report, together with separate and supplementary views, 90th Congress, 2nd Session, July 30, 31, and August 1, 1968. Washington, D. C., Government Printing Office, 1968.

U. S. Congress. Joint Economic Committee. Subcommittee on Economy in Government.
Interest rate guidelines for federal decision making, Hearing, 90th Congress, 2nd session, January 29, 1968. Washington D. C., Government Printing, Office 1968.

U. S. Congress. Joint Economic Committee. Subcommittee on Economy in Government.
Planning-programming-budgeting system: progress and potentials. Hearings, 90th Congress, 1st session, September 14, 19, 21, 1967. Washington, D. C., Government Printing Office, 1967. 412 p.

U. S. Congress. Joint Economic Committee. Subcommittee on Economy in Government.

Subcommittee report on economic analysis of public investment decisions: interest rate policy and discounting analysis. 90th Congress, 2nd session, September 23, 1968. Washington, D. C., Government Printing Office, 1968.

U. S. Congress. Joint Economic Committee. Subcommittee on Economy in Government.
Subcommittee report on the planning-programming-budgeting system: progress and potentials, 90th Congress, 1st session, December 4, 1967. Washington D. C., Government Printing Office, 1968.

U. S. Congress. Senate. Committee on Government Operations.
Financial management in the federal government, volume II. Washington D. C., Government Printing Office, 1971. 491 p. (Senate Document 92-50).

U. S. Congress. Senate. Committee on Government Operations. Subcommittee on Intergovernmental Relations.
Criteria for evaluation in planning state and local programs, a study, prepared by Harry P. Hatry, 90th Congress, 1st session, July 21, 1967. Washington D. C., Government Printing Office, 1967.

U. S. Congress. Senate. Committee on Government Operations. Subcommittee on National Security and International Operations.
Planning-programming-budgeting: inquiry, Senator Henry M. Jackson, Chairman. 90th and 91st Congress, 1st session, March, 1970, Washington, D. C., Government Printing Office, 1970. 683 p. (This publication draws together the findings of the sub-committee's two-year inquiry into PPBS. Contains a wealth of information.)

U. S. Dept. of Agriculture. Office of the Secretary.
Planning-programming-budgeting system. Secretary's memorandum, no. 1965. 5 p.

U. S. Dept. of Defense.
A primer on Project PRIME. Washington D. C., Dec. 1966. 78 p.

U. S. Dept. of Defense. Office of the Assistant Secretary of Defense (Comptroller). Prime 69. Denver, 1968.

U. S. Dept. of Health, Education and Welfare.
Planning-programming-budgeting: guidance for program and financial plan. rev. ed. Washington D. C., Government Printing Office, February 1968. 207 p.

U. S. Dept. of Health, Education and Welfare.
Program Analysis. Washington, D. C., 1966-1968. 14 nos.

U. S. Dept of Health, Education and Welfare. Education Office.
Statewide long-range planning for libraries, report of conference, September 19-22, 1965, Chicago, Illinois, sponsored by Library Services Branch; edited by Herbert A. Carl. Washington, D. C., 1966. 59 p.

U. S. Dept. of the Treasury. Library.
Planning-programming-systems: a collection of bibliographies. Washington, D. C., 1968.

U. S. Dept. of the Treasury. Library.
Planning-programming-budgeting systems. Special readings
collated by the Staff of the Treasury Department.
Washington, D. C., 1968.

U. S. General Accounting Office.
Glossary for systems analysis and planning, programming,
budgeting. Washington, D. C.,
Government Printing Office, 1969. 72 p.

U. S. Library of Congress. Legislative Reference Service.
The planning-programming-budgeting system: an annotated
bibliography, by Robert L. Chartrand and Dennis W. Brezina.
Washington D. C., 1967. 23 p.

U. S. President's Commission on Budget Concepts.
Report. Washington D. C., Government Printing Office,
1967, 109 p.

U. S. President's Commission on Budget Concepts.
Staff papers and other materials. Washington D. C.,
Government Printing Office, October 1967. 512 p.

U. S. President's Commission on the National Goals.
Goals for Americans. Englewood Cliffs, New Jersey,
Prentice-Hall, 1960.

Washington State Library.
Performance budgeting bibliography including planning-
programming-budgeting. Olympia, Washington State Library,
1969. 6 p.

Washington, University. Department of Economics.
Planning-programming-budgeting systems: selected case
materials, by Murray L. Weidenbaum. St. Louis, 1969.

Washington, University. Institute of Public Affairs.
Performance budgeting in agency management; workshop in
public management. Seattle, 1962. 66 p.

Weidenbaum, Murray L. and John S. Salome, III.
Congress and the federal budget. Washington, D. C., American
Enterprise Institute for Public Policy Research, 1965.

Weidenbaum, Murray L.
A government-wide program budget. Institute for Urban and
Regional Studies, St. Louis, Washington University, 1967. 11 p.

Wildavsky, Aaron.
The politics of the budgetary process. Boston, Little, Brown, 1964.

GENERAL BACKGROUND AND HISTORY

Periodical Articles

ACCOUNTING REVIEW
Bierman, Harold, Jr.
"A use of probability and statistics in performance evaluation."
July 1961, p. 409-417. (Describes a quantitative model for solving
the decision problem of when to investigate a variance.)

AIR UNIVERSITY REVIEW
Peterson, Robert L.
"The use and misuse of cost-effectiveness." Vol. 17, March-
April 1966, p. 81-84.

AMERICAN JOURNAL OF AGRICULTURAL ECONOMICS
Kelso, Maurice M.
"Public land policy in the contex of PPB systems."
Vol. 50, December 1968, p. 167-186.

AMERICAN INSTITUTE OF PLANNERS, JOURNAL
Hill, Morris.
"A goals-achievement matrix for evaluating plans." Vol. 34,
January 1968, p. 19-29. (Examines some established techniques
of plan evaluation by cost-benefit analysis).

Millward, Robert E.
"PPBS: problems of implementation." Vol. 34, March 1968,
p. 88-94. (Asserts that PPBS has inherent conceptual weaknesses,
poses operational problems, and is antithetical to present institutional and organizational practices).

Page, David A.
"The federal planning-programming-budgeting system."
Vol. 33, July 1967, p. 256-259. (Gives an optimistic opinion of
the value of PPBS for government programs).

Seidman, David R.
"PPB in HEW: some management issues." Vol. 36, May 1970,
p. 168-178. (Discusses such issues as inter-agency conflicts and
measurement problems).

Vedder, James.
"Planning problems with multidimensional consequences." Vol.
36, March 1970, p. 112-119. (Proposes an approach to simplify
the final decision problem).

AMERICAN POLITICAL SCIENCE REVIEW
Davis, Otto, M. A. H. Dempster and Aaron Wildavsky.
"A theory of the budgeting process." Vol. 60, September 1966,
p. 529-547. (Presents a rather technical discussion of the federal
budgetary process and suggests simple models to represent basic
features of the process).

Hammond, Paul Y.
"A functional analysis of Defense Department decision-making
in the McNamara administration." Vol. 62. March 1968, p. 57-69.
(Assesses the effect of PPBS on the bureaucratic politics of the
Defense Department).

ANNALS OF AMERICAN ACADEMY OF POLITICAL
AND SOCIAL SCIENCE
Zwick, Charles J.
"Budgeting for federal responsibilities." September 1968,
p. 13-21. (Relates PPBS to the federal budget).

ARIZONA REVIEW
Tansik, David A.
"Trends in Pentagon budgeting and contracting policies."
Vol. 20, April 1971, p. 10-17.

ARMED FORCES MANAGEMENT
Heiman, Grover.
"Defense reverses PPB process." February 1970, p. 43-45.
"Is PPBS all that good?"
April 1968, p. 32-33.

BANKING
Proxmire, William.
"PPBS — a new approach to government spending." Vol. 61,
February 1969 p. 39+. (An interview with Senator Proxmire in
which he endorses application of PPBS to government spending).

BUDGETING
Karsh, Norman.
"PPBS: for better or for worse." May/June 1968, p. 11-14.
(Analyzes the problems of implementing PPBS and concludes
that PPBS can be for "better").

BUSINESS AND GOVERNMENT REVIEW
Weidenbaum, Murray L.
"Program budgeting: applying economic analysis to government
expenditure decisions." Vol. 7, July/August 1966, p. 22-31.

BUSINESS HORIZONS
Novick, David.
"Long-range planning through program budgeting." Vol. 12,
February 1969, p. 59-65. (Asserts that PPB provides for better
use of existing resources).
Steiner, George A.
"Program budgeting: business contribution to government
management." Spring 1965, p. 43-52. (Advises managers to be
ready to accept program budgeting, since it will greatly enhance
efficiency in government).

BUSINESS QUARTERLY
Oliphant, Peter.
"Program definition in PPBS." Vol. 35, Summer 1970, p. 72-77.
(Discusses the application of programming to corporate
planning needs).

CALIFORNIA MANAGEMENT REVIEW
Novick, David.
"The origin and history of program budgeting." Vol. 11,

Fall 1968, p. 7-12. (Provides excellent background to the development of PPBS).

CANADIAN CHARTERED ACCOUNTANT
McNicoll, J. A.
"Programme planning and operation analysis." Vol. 91, October 1967, p. 277-279. (Supplies a good introduction to PPBS along with an example of application).
Ross, N. G.
"Toward better control of federal government expenditures." Feb. 1969, p. 100-103. (Asserts that program budgeting is working well for the federal government and merits wider application).

CANADIAN OPERATIONAL RESEARCH SOCIETY .JOURNAL.
Jamieson, D. M.
"Program planning and budgeting in the Federal government." Vol. 7, 1969, p. 116-124.

CANADIAN PUBLIC ADMINISTRATION
Cutt, James.
"Efficiency and effectiveness in public sector spending: the programme budgeting approach." 1970, p. 396-426.
Fowke, Donald V.
"PPB for provinces." 1969, p. 72-77.

CANADIAN STATISTICAL REVIEW
Bolton, W. B.
"Government finance statistics and their relevance to program planning budget systems." August 1968, p. ii-v. (Describes the use of various budget statistics in PPBS).

CIVIL SERVICE JOURNAL
Rowen, Henry S.
"PPBS: what and why." Jan.-Mar. 1966, p. 5-9. (Explains why PPBS was introduced throughout federal government).
Wright, Chester.
CSC provides PPBS training." Jan.-Mar. 1966, p. 10, 11, 14. (Describes the Civil Service Commission's three-week in-residence PPBS Seminar).

CONFERENCE BOARD RECORD
Levy, Michael E.
"Planning-programming-budgeting: government's new tool for improving efficiency." Vol. 4, May 1967, p. 41-43. (Describes the federal PPB system).

COST AND MANAGEMENT
"Management accounting for government."
September 1967 through February 1968 issues. (Describes PPBS with special emphasis on accounting).

CANADIAN TAX JOURNAL
Benson, E. J.
"Budget breakthrough: adoption of PPB." Vol. 16, May/June 1968, p. 161-167.

CERTIFIED GENERAL ACCOUNTANT
Faulkner, Paul J.
"A systems approach to programming." Oct. 1967, p. 19-27.

CHALLENGE
Chamberlain, Neil W.
"Government investment: how scientific can it be?" Vol. 14, July/August 1966, p. 32-44. (Implies that cost-benefit analysis, valuable as it may be, is not a substitute for human judgement).

DATAMATION
Hitch, Charles J.
"Program budgeting." Vol. 13, September 1967, p. 37-40. (Outlines development of PPBS and some of the problems, risks, and opportunities involved in its application).

ECONOMIC AND BUSINESS BULLETIN (Temple University)
Sheppard, William J.
"Planning-programming-budgeting system: a review." Vol. 23. Winter 1971, p. 21-28. (Reviews experience in the U. S. Defense Department, controversy over PPB as an abstract concept, and experience with it on a government-wide basis).

ECONOMIC JOURNAL (London)
Turvey, Ralph.
"Present value versus internal rate of return: an essay in the theory of third best." Vol. 73, March 1963, p. 92-98. (Discusses the formulation of criteria for use in determining the size and composition of public investment programmes).
Feldstein, Martin S.
"The social time preference discount rate in cost benefit analysis." Vol. 74, June 1964, p. 360-379. (Examines method of determining social benefits versus cost of public investments).
Prest, A. R. and R. Turvey.
"Cost-benefit analysis: a survey." Vol. 75, December 1965, p. 683-735. (Discusses general principles as well as particular applications).

ECONOMIST
"Budget in peril."
Vol. 233, November 22, 1969, p. 52. (Points out that any sort of planning is hampered until Congress has spoken on the budget).
"Civil service; all do PAR."
Vol. 238, February 6, 1971, p. 69. (Discusses PAR (programme analysis and review), the British equivalent of PPB, which seems more palatable to them, now that they have their own acronym).
"Callaghan's good deed."
Vol. 232, July 19, 1969, p. 21+. (Examines the British governments' experiments with PPBS).

FEDERAL ACCOUNTANT
Bayer, Sylvan.
"PPBS - a new management tool." Vol. 17, December 1968, p.

82-90. (Reviews the use of PPBS by the executive branch of the government in the two years following President Johnson's directive that the system be installed).

Botner, Stanley B.
"The Bureau of the Budget's effort to integrate PPB and traditional appropriation processes." Vol. 19, June 1970, p. 108-113. (Describes McKinsey & Co., Inc. efforts to assist the Bureau of the Budget in this endeavor).

Botner, Stanley B.
"Implementing PPBS: Bureau of the Budget; integrated system development effort." Vol. 18, June 1969, p. 95-101. (Introduces readers to the efforts of the McKinsey management consultants to design an information system to support and help integrate BOB's PPBS).

Harrill, E. Reece.
"Performance budgeting and accounting." Vol. 14, Spring 1965, p. 35-58. (Stresses the importance of budgeting and accounting in management).

Morse, Elsworth H., Jr.
"The planning-programming-budgeting system and the Congress." Vol. 18, September 1969, p. 23-36. (Examines the attitudes of various Congressional committees toward PPBS).

Posner, Ben.
"Planning-programming-budgeting; a financial management approach." Vol. 15, Summer 1966, p. 9-21. (Analyzes the new PPBS in terms of its impact on the Federal government).

Simmons, Brigadier General Edward H. USMC.
"Planners, programmers, and budgeters." Vol. 18, September 1969, p. 37-53. (Questions how well PPBS is meeting the needs of the Marine Corps).

G. A. O. REVIEW
Staats, Elmer B.
"The relationship of budgeting program planning and evaluation." Winter 1970, p. 3-10. (Based on remarks presented at the Budget Analysts Institute, Chapel Hill, N. C., August 20, 1969).

GEORGIA BUSINESS
Lee, Sang M.
"Program budgeting: a tool for management."
Vol. 29, September 1969, p. 1-5.

HARVARD BUSINESS REVIEW
Granger, Charles H.
"The hierarchy of objectives." Vol. 42, May/June 1964, p. 63-74. (Stresses the importance of defining objectives).

Macleod, Roderick K.
"Program budgeting works in nonprofit institutions: cost accounting of professional services pinpoints sources and uses of funds and facilitates decisions on money allocation."
Vol. 49, Sept./Oct. 1971, p. 46-56.

Novick, David.
The federal budget as a business indicator." May/June 1960,
p. 64-72. (Recommends changes to render the federal budget
more useful as a planning instrument for businessman and
economists).

INDIAN JOURNAL OF PUBLIC ADMINISTRATION
Viswonathan, S. S.
"Performance budgeting in India: a review of the developments,
present status and prospects." Vol. 16, April/June 1970,
p. 188-202.

INTERNATIONAL REVIEW OF ADMINISTRATIVE SCIENCES
Jacqmotte, J. P.
"Tentative comparative study of RCB in France and PPBS in
Belgium." Vol. 36, 1970, p. 47-55.

JOURNAL OF ACCOUNTANCY
"Elements of program budgeting."
Vol. 131, April 1971, p. 84-86. (Describes the six major elements
of PPBS: 1) program structuring, 2) strategic planning, 3) programming, 4) budgeting, 5) information and reporting systems,
and 6) program control and evaluation).
King, Barry G.
"Cost-effectiveness analysis: implications for accountants." Vol.
129, March 1970, p. 43-49. (Explains cost-effectiveness analysis
in nontechnical terms).

JOURNAL OF POLITICS
Jernberg, James E.
"Information change and congressional behavior: a caveat for
PPB reformers." Vol. 31, August 1969, p. 722-740. (Warns of
some of the implications of PPBS).

JOURNAL OF SYSTEMS MANAGEMENT
Berg, R. D.
"Systems help educational planning and control." Vol. 21, Decem-
ber 1970, p. 8-14. (Describes experience in the California edu-
cational system).
Horton, F. W., Jr.
"Building block approach: key to federal management systems?"
Vol. 22, October 1971, p. 38-41.

LAND ECONOMICS
Devine, Eugene J.
"Treatment of incommensurables in cost-benefit analysis." Vol.
42, Aug. 1966, p. 383-387. (Attempts to clarify the applicability
and limitations of cost-benefit analysis).

LOCAL GOVERNMENT FINANCE (London)
Cox, B. E.
"Performance budgeting with particular reference to highway
maintenance: towards the implementation of the Marshall re-
port of highway maintenance (Great Britain). Vol. 75,
November 1971, p. 390-396.

Rose, K. E.
"Management processes and systems development (program budgeting as a management system)." Vol. 74, October 1970, p. 338-342.

LONG RANGE PLANNING
Dougharty, L. A.
"Developing corporate strategy through planning, programming, and budgeting." Vol. 2, March 1970, p. 24-29.
Fisher, G. H.
"The world of program budgeting." Vol. 2, September 1969, p. 50-60.

MANAGEMENT ACCOUNTING
Nichols, D. R.
"PPBS: a challenge to non-profit accounting." Vol. 51, November 1969, p. 12-13. (Asserts that PPBS offers a number of advantages in the non-profit decision-making process).

MANAGEMENT CONTROLS
Elkin, Robert.
"Applying PPBS to public welfare." Vol. 16, November 1969, p. 237-242. (Discusses and questions use of PPBS, with particular reference to public welfare. See also his article on p. 18 of January 1969 issue).
Graese, C. E.
"Defining PPBS." Vol. 16, November 1969, p. 235-236. (Provides a brief, but thought-provoking definition).
Graese, C. F.
"Program budgeting for government." Vol. 14, September 1967, p. 201-202.

MANAGEMENT IN GOVERNMENT
Dean, Alan L.
"Planning, programming and budgeting in the United States." Vol. 1, Oct./Dec. 1969, p. 67-80.

MANAGEMENT REVIEW
Murphy, Joseph S.
"Planning, programming and budgeting: the quiet revolution in government planning techniques." Vol. 57, No. 4, April 1968, p. 4-11.

MAYOR AND MANAGER
Bopp, K. D.
"Planning-programming-budgeting." Vol. 11, No. 5, May 1968, p. 6-8.
Schaller, Lyle E.
"Make your budget work for you! PPBS and other budget techniques." February 1969, p. 17-21. (Compares capital budgeting, performance budgeting and PPBS, including application to the library).

MUNICIPAL YEARBOOK, 1968
Hatry, Harry P.
"Systems analysis and PPBS." Vol. 35, 1968, p. 273-279.
(Provides an overview of the history, definitions, expectations, and problems of PPBS).

NATURAL RESOURCES JOURNAL
Hammond, Richard J.
"Convention and limitation in benefit-cost analysis." Vol. 6, April 1966, p. 195-222. (Analyzes conventional use and limitations)

NATIONAL TAX JOURNAL
Escarraz, Donald Ray.
"PPBS and the national government: alternative approaches." Vol. 21, June 1968, p. 130-140. (Presents four alternative approaches: fiscal policy approach, welfare economics approach, systems approach, and systematic approach).

NEW ZEALAND JOURNAL OF PUBLIC ADMINISTRATION
Laking, R., tr.
"A new approach to financial management."
Vol. 32, 1969, p. 39-49.

O & M BULLETIN
Bridgeman, J. M.
"Planning-programming-budgeting systems."
Fall 1969, p. 167-178.
Bridgeman, J. M.
"Planning-programming-budgeting systems II."
Vol. 25, 1970, p. 16-27.
Wasserman, G. J.
"Planning-programming-budgeting in the police service in England and Wales." Vol. 25, May 1970, p. 197-210.

OPTIMUM
Harris, Derek D.
"Performance measurement in government."
Vol. 1, No. 3, 1970, p. 52-61.

PERSONNEL ADMINISTRATION
Greenhouse, Samuel M.
"A 'distributed output' concept for the planning-programming-budgeting system." Vol. 30, July/August 1967, p. 35-41. (Predicts great utility for PPBS if properly implemented by the federal government).
Rosen, Bernard.
"The personnel director, program planning and budgeting." Vol. 29, Sept./Oct. 1966, p. 3-5. (Outlines the personnel director's responsibilities with regard to PPBS in federal government).

PLANNING
American Society of Planning Officials.
"Planning-programming-budgeting system: tool for breakthrough." 1967, p. 81-99. (Contents: A local government approach

to a planning-programming-budgeting system, by Donald H. Blatt. — Some perspective on federal PPBS, by William B. Ross. — PPBS and the evolution of planning, by Anthony Downs).

PUBLIC ADMINISTRATION REVIEW

Botner, Stanley B.
"Four Years of PPBS: an appraisal." Vol. 30, July/August 1970, p. 423-431. (The author is disappointed with the results of PPBS in federal agencies yet feels it has potential).

Dror, Yehezkel.
"Policy analysts; a new professional role in government service." Vol. 27, September 1967, p. 197-203. (Emphasizes need for qualitative and political analysis, rather than nearly exclusive preoccupation with quantitative methods).

Gorham, William.
"Sharpening the knife that cuts the public pie." Vol. 28, May/June 1968, p. 236-241. (Reviews the impact of PPB on the Department of Health, Education, and Welfare).

Harper, Edwin L., Fred A. Kramer and Andrew M. Rouse.
"Implementation and use of PPB in sixteen federal agencies." Vol. 29, Nov./Dec. 1969, p. 623-632. (Reports the findings of a Bureau of the Budget study).

Howard, S. Kenneth.
"The PPB game." Vol. 30, March/April 1970, p. 193-194. (Reviews four books on PPB).

McGilvery, Francis E.
"Program and responsibility cost accounting." Vol. 28, March/April 1968, p. 148-154. (Discusses some implications of PPB to accounting practices).

Massey, Robert J.
"Program packages and the program budgeting in the Department of Defense." Vol. 23, March 1963, p. 30.34. (Provides an early look at PPBS in the Department of Defense).

"Performance budgeting: has the theory worked?"
Vol. 20, Spring 1960, p. 63-85. (Contents: Performance budgeting in Los Angeles, by Ali Eghtedari and Frank Sherwood. — New York state's performance budget experiment, by Marion L. Henry and Willis Proctor. — USDA's pioneering performance budget, by Ralph S. Roberts. — Cincinnati's budget developments, by Vernon E. Koch).

PUBLIC ADMINISTRATION REVIEW

"Planning-programming-budgeting system: a symposium."
Vol. 26, December 1966, p. 243-310. (Contents: The road to PPB: the stages of budget reform, by Allen Schick. — Toward federal program budgeting, by Werner Z. Hirsch. — The planning-programming-budgeting system: rationale, language, and idea-relationships, by Samuel Greenhouse. — A management accounts structure, by Francis E. McGilvery. — The program budget and the interest rate for public investment, by Robert L. Banks and Arnold Katz. — The political economy of efficiency: cost

benefit analysis, systems analysis and program budgeting, by Aaron Wildavsky).

"Planning-programming-budgeting system reexamined: development analysis and criticism."

Vol. 29, March/April 1969, p. 111-202. (Contents: The new systems budgeting, by Allen Schick. — PPB and the public policy-making system: some reflections on the papers by Bertram M. Gross and Allen Schick, by Yehezkel Dror. — PPB and state budgeting, by William M. Capron. — Limitations and problems of PPBS in the states, by Frederick C. Mosher. — PPB in cities, by Selma J. Mushkin. — PPB; how can it be implemented? by C. W. Churchman and A. H. Schainblatt. — Rescuing policy analysis from PPBS, by Aaron Wildavsky. Emphasizes criticism).

PUBLIC FINANCE
Feldstein, Martin S.
"Opportunity cost calculations in cost-benefit analysis." Vol. 19, No. 2, 1964, p. 117-139.

PUBLIC INTEREST
Brzezinski, Zbigniew.
"Purpose and planning in foreign policy." No. 14, Winter 1969, p. 52-73.
"Economics and public policy."
No. 12, Summer 1968, p. 68-118. (Contents: The economic approach to social questions, by Marry G. Johnson. — Model makers and decision makers: economists and the policy process, by Carl Kaysen. — Economics, sociology, and the best of all possible worlds, by Mancur Olson, Jr.).
Held, Virginia.
"PPBS comes to Washington." Summer 1966, p. 102-115.
"PPBS: its scope and limits."
No. 8, Summer 1967, p. 3-48. (Contents: Notes of a practioner, by William Gorham. — HEW grapples with PPBS, by Elizabeth Drew. — The political economy of efficiency, by Aaron Wildavsky).
Schelling, Thomas C.
"PPBS and foreign affairs." No. 11, Spring 1968, p. 26-36. (Surmises that PPBS may be valuable — depending on the expertise of those implementing it — in the field of foreign affairs).

QUARTERLY JOURNAL OF ECONOMICS
Maass, Arthur.
"Benefit-cost analysis: its relevance to public expenditure decisions." Vol. 80, May 1966, p. 208-226. (Examines and evaluates benefit-cost analysis).

REGIONAL SCIENCE ASSOCIATION PAPERS
Burns, Leland S.
"Cost-benefit analysis of a social overhead project for regional development." Vol. 16, 1965, p. 155-161.
Hirsch, Werner Z.

"State and local government program budgeting." Vol. 18, 1967, p. 147-163.

SCOTTISH JOURNAL OF POLITICAL ECONOMY
Gillhespy, N. R.
"The Tay road bridge: a case study in cost-benefit analysis." Vol. 15, 1968, p. 167-183. (Discusses the case in considerable detail).

SOCIO-ECONOMIC PLANNING SCIENCES
Sisson, Roger L., et al.
"The project concept in planning, programming and budgeting." Vol. 4, 1970, p. 239-261.

WELFARE IN REVIEW
Levine, Abraham S.
"Cost-benefit analysis and social welfare." Vol 4, Feb. 1966, p. 1-11. (Explores possible applications).
Levine Abraham S.
"Cost-benefit analysis of the work experience program." Vol. 4, Aug./Sept. 1966, p. 1-9. (Delineates a research plan for cost-benefit analysis of the Aid to Families with Dependent Children program).
Spindler, Arthur.
"PPBS and social and rehabilitation services." Vol. 7, March/April 1969, p. 22-28. (Reviews HEW use of PPBS and predicts success in applying it to social and rehabilitation programs).

ZEITSCHRIFT FÜR DIE GESAMTE STAATSWISSENSCHAFT
Stolber, Walter B.
"The objective function in program budgeting: some basic outlines." Vol. 127. May 1971, p. 213-229.

APPLICATIONS TO STATE AND LOCAL GOVERNMENT

Monographs

Airlie House Institute on University Training, 1969.
University training in PPB for state and local officials.
Washington D. C., Urban Institute, 1970. 93 p.

Bales, Carter F.
Implementing PPBS in the City of New York. Chicago,
Municipal Finance Officers Association of the United States
and Canada, 1969.

Bishop, Warren.
Washington's new fiscal management system. Olympia, Central
Budget Agency, State of Washington, 1959. 12 p.

Briggs, John F.
A refined program budget for state governments. Washington,
D. C., American University. School of Government and Public
Administration, 1962. 45 p.

California. Dept. of Finance Management.
Conversion to the programming and budgeting system.
Sacramento, 1966. Memo no. 66-14. (Related memos: 66-16,
66-17, and 66-31).

California. Dept. of Finance Management.
Programming and budgeting system. Sacramento, 1969.

California. University. Institute of Governmental Affairs.
Program and budgeting systems conference. Davis,
California, 1969.

Carlson, William A.
A report and recommendations on planning, programming, and
budgeting for agriculture in the State of Hawaii. Honolulu, 1969.

Chicago. Home Rule Commission.
Modernizing a city government. Chicago, University of Chicago
Press, 1954.

Consolidated Analysis Center, Inc.
Application of planning-programming-budgeting systems
(PPBS) to state government. Santa Monica, California, 1969.

Council of State Governments.
The integration of planning and budgeting in the states.
Lexington, Kentucky, 1969.

Council of State Governments.
State progress in planning and budgeting systems.
Lexington, Kentucky, 1969.

Council of State Governments.
State reports on five-five-five: a pilot project on planning-
programming-budgeting systems. Chicago, 1968. 32 p.

Devine, Eugene J.
State and local program budgeting: problems and prospects.
Paper presented at the annual Southern California Institute on
Government, California State College at Los Angeles, June 15-16,
1967. Los Angeles, California State College, 1967. 15 p.

Fairfax Co., Va. Board of County Supervisors.
Planning, programming, budgeting. Fairfax, Virginia, 1967. 15 p.

Florida. Legislative Auditor. Management Systems Division.
Evolving concepts in Florida: performance audits and program budgets. Papers presented to the 21st annual Legislative Conference, Miami Beach, Florida, August 22, 1968, by Ernest Ellison and staff members. Tallahassee, Florida, 1968.
Gabis, Stanley T.
Mental Health and Financial Management: some dilemmas of program budgeting. East Lansing, Michigan State University, 1960. 68 p.
George Washington University. Department of Economics.
Planning-programming-budgeting systems: selected case materials. Washington, D. C., 1969.
George Washington University. State-Local Finances Project.
Criteria for evaluation in planning state and local programs. Washington, D. C., 1967. 52 p.
George Washington University. State-Local Finances Project.
Criteria for program selection, by Harry P. Hatry, Washington D. C., 1968.
George Washington University. State-Local Finances Project.
Functional federalism: grants-in-aid and PPB system, by Selma Mushkin, John F. Cotton and Gabrielle C. Lupo. Washington D. C., 1968. 208 p.
George Washington University. State-Local Finances Project.
Implementing PPB in state, city, and county, by Selma Mushkin and others. Washington D. C., 1969. 159 p. (Evaluates the project in which PPB was applied for a 12-month trial period to 5 states, 5 counties, and 5 cities).
George Washington University. State-Local Finances Project.
Long-range revenue estimation, by Eugene P. McLoone, Gabrielle C. Lupo and Selma J. Mushkin. Washington, D. C., 1967. 122 p.
George Washington University. State-Local Finances Project.
An operative PPB system: a collaborative undertaking in the states, by Selma J. Mushkin and M. Willcox. Washington D. C., 1968. 24 p.
George Washington University. State-Local Finances Project.
PPB pilot project reports from the participating 5 states, 5 counties, and 5 cities. Washington, February 1969. (States: California, Michigan, New York, Vermont, Wisconsin. Counties: Dade, Florida; Los Angeles; Nashville-Davidson; Nassau; Wayne, Michigan; Cities: Dayton, Ohio; Denver, Detroit, New Haven, San Diego. Covers period, July 1967 - July 31, 1968).
George Washington University. State-Local Finances Project.
Planning-programming-budgeting for City, State, County obtives, PPB notes. Washington D. C., 1967-1968. 11 vols. Contents: Note 1. Answering the question: is an integrated planning, programming, budgeting system useful for our jurisdiction? 2. Administrative framework for establishing planning-programming systems in states, cities, and counties: some considerations and suggested possibilities. 3. Development of initial instructions to inaugurate a planning-programming-budgeting system: some

preliminary considerations and model instruction to be adapted for local use. 4. Problems of staffing and training for a PPB system in state and local governments. 5. Development of output-oriented program structure. 6. Role and nature of cost analysis in a PPB system. 7. Output measures for a PPB system, multi-year program and financial plan. 8. The multi-year program and financial plan. 9. Demographic and economic data guidelines for a PPB system. 10. Program objectives, effectiveness criteria, and program structure - an illustration for highway safety. 11. A first step to analysis: the issue paper.

George Washington University. State-Local Finances Project.
Program planning for state, county, city, by Harry P. Hatry and John F. Cotton. Washington, D. C., 1967.

George Washington University. State-Local Finances Project.
The search for alternatives: program options in a PPB system, by Selma Mushkin and Brian Herman.
Washington D. C., 1968. 66p.

George Washington University. State-Local Finances Project.
What is PPB? Planning-programming-budgeting for city, state, county objectives. Washington D. C., 1967. 8 p.

Greaney, Walter T.
A program budget for Massachusetts. University of Massachusetts. Bureau of Governmental Research. 1962. 36 p.

Hawaii. Legislature. Office of the Legislative Auditor.
The planning-programming-budgeting system and Hawaii's program budget: a comparison. Honolulu, 1967.

Hawaii. Legislature. Office of the Legislative Auditor.
Transcript of seminar in planning-programming-budgeting for the State of Hawaii, held January 30 - February 2, 1968.
Honolulu, 1968.

Hawaii. University.
Training guide on program budgeting. Honolulu, 1966. Contents: No. 2-A, the program memorandum. — No. 2-B, Program structure and evaluation. — No. 2-C, University of California program budgeting training materials.

Hirsch, Werner Z.
State and local government program budgeting. Paper prepared for the 6th European Congress of the Regional Science Assn., Vienna, Austria, August 31, 1966. Los Angeles, Institute of Government and Public Affairs, University of California, 1966.

Knighton, Lennis M.
The performance post audit in state government: an analysis of its nature, its purpose, and its possibility. East Lansing, Michigan, Bureau of Business and Economic Research, Division of Research, Graduate School of Business Administration, Michigan State University, 1967.

McGown, Wayne F.
How to apply program-planning-budgeting to your state. Address delivered at National Conference of State Legislators, Washington, D. C., December 6, 1966. Madison, Wisconsin, Bureau of

Management, Department of Administration,
State of Wisconsin , 1966.

Management Analysis Center, Inc.
Teaching cases in planning-programming-budgeting for state
and local governments, prepared by Graeme M. Taylor and Richard J. Gill on behalf of the Ford Foundation and the State-
Local Finances Project, George Washington University.
Washington D. C., 1969.

Melone, R. J.
Resource analysis model for the Arkansas State Police.
Santa Monica, Rand Corp., 1970. 105 p.

Michigan. Dept. of State.
A state agency impression of the program budgeting approach,
by George O. Stevens and Charles O. Durocher.
Lansing, 1967. 12 p.

Mowitz, Robert J.
The design and implementation of Pennsylvania's planning, programming, budgeting system. Harrisburg, Pennsylvania, Publications Bureau, Pennsylvania Dept. of Property and Supplies,
1970. 72 p.

Mushkin, Selma.
State programming and economic development. Lexington,
Kentucky, Council of State Governments, 1965.

National Association of State Budget Officers.
The budget analyst in state management, a partial record of
NASBO Institute for Management Analysis held at the University of Kentucky, July 23 - August 3, 1967.
Lexington, Kentucky, Council of State Governments, 1968.

National Association of State Budget Officers.
Budgeting for responsible state government, a partial record
of the National Association of State Budget Officers Institute for
Budget Analysts held at Syracuse University, July 21-26, 1968.
Lexington, Kentucky, Council of State Governments, 1969.

National Association of State Budget Officers.
Budgets for state planning. Proceedings of NASBO Budget on
State Planning held at Boulder, Colorado, June, 1968.
Lexington, Kentucky, Council of State Governments, 1969.

National Association of State Budget Officers.
Central budget analyst in state government, a partial record
of NASBO Institute for Budget Analysts held at the University
of Kentucky, July 9-14, 1967. Lexington, Kentucky,
Council of State Governments, 1968.

National Association of State Budget Officers.
Management role of state budget analyst, a partial record of
the National Association of State Budget Officers Institute for
Management Analysis held at the University of Kentucky,
September 25-30, 1966. Lexington, Kentucky, Council of State
Governments, 1967. 133 p.

National Association of State Budget Officers.
State program budgeting: possibilities and limitations. Proceed-

ing of NASBO Institute for Budget Directors at Natural Bridge
State Park, September 17-22, 1967. Lexington, Kentucky,
Council of State Governments, 1968.
NASBO Institute on Natural Resources, University of Kentucky,
1968. State budgeting for natural resources programs. National
Association of State Budget Officers, 1968. 67 p.
National Governor's Conference. Committee on Executive Manage-
ment and Fiscal Affairs. Advisory Task Force.
The integration of planning and budgeting in the United States.
Lexington, Kentucky, Council of State Governments, 1969.
New York, Division of the Budget. Office of Planning
Coordination.
Guidelines for integrated planning programming, budgeting.
Albany, 1968. 75 p.
Schick, Allen.
Budget innovation in the States. Washington,
Brookings Institution, 1971. 223 p.
Stevens, George O. and Charles O. Durocher.
A state agency impression of the program budgeting approach.
Detroit, Office of Driver and Vehicle Services,
Michigan Department of State, May 1967.
U. S. Bureau of the Budget. Federal Technical Assistance Team.
Strengthening planning, programming, and budgeting in the
Colorado government. Washington, D. C., 1969.
U. S. Congress. Joint Economic Committee. Subcommittee on
Economy in Government.
Innovations in planning, programming, and budgeting in state
and local governments. A compendium of papers.
91st Congress, 1st session, Washington, D. C., Government
Printing Office, 1969. 218 p.
U. S. Congress. Joint Economic Committee. Subcommittee on
Economy in Government.
Planning-programming-budgeting system: progress and
potentials. Hearings, 90th Congress, 1st session,
September 14, 18, 21, 1967. Washington D. C.,
Government Printing Office, 1967. 412 p.
U. S. Congress. Senate. Committee on Appropriations.
Subcommittee on D. C. Appropriations.
D. C. Appropriations for fiscal year 1971. Hearings,
91st Congress, 2nd session, March 19, 1970.
Washington, D. C., 1970. p. 207-218.
U. S. Congress. Senate. Committee on Governments Operations.
Subcommittee on Intergovernmental Relations.
Criteria for evaluation in planning state and local programs,
by Harry P. Hatry. Washington, D. C., Government Printing
Office, 1967. 42 p. (90th Congress, 1st session, committee print).
U. S. Office of the Vice President.
The Vice-President's handbook for local officials; a guide to
Federal assistance for local governments. Washington, D. C.,
Government Printing Office, 1967. 297 p.

U. S. Urban Management Assistance Administration.
Capital improvements programming in local government.
Washington, D. C., 1969.
Wisconsin, Dept. of Administration. Bureau of Management.
A prospective integrated planning-budgeting system for
Wisconsin State Government. Madison, December 1967. 15 p.
Wisconsin. Dept. of Administration. Bureau of Personnel.
Planning, budget and management analysis. Madison, 1968.
Wisconsin. Dept. of Administration. Bureau of Management.
Wisconsin's conversion to program budgeting, by Paul L. Brown,
Executive Budget Co-Ordinator. Wichita, Kansas,
December 1, 1966. 24 p.

APPLICATIONS TO STATE & LOCAL GOVERNMENT

Periodical Articles

AMERICAN CITY
Shannon, George C.
"Defining work units for performance budgets."
May 1956, p. 191-195. (A guide for reducing complex municipal
operations to a series of work units).

AMERICAN JOURNAL OF PUBLIC HEALTH
Berkowitz, Monroe.
"PPBS, state-wide planning and the goals of vocational reha-
bilitation". Sept. 1968, p. 1633-1637. (Discusses application of
PPBS to vocational rehabilitation programs in realistic terms).

ANNALS OF THE AMERICAN ACADEMY OF POLITICAL
AND SOCIAL SCIENCES
Crihfield, Brerard and George A. Bell.
"Budgeting for state and local government service." Sept. 1968,
p. 31-38. (Discusses applications of PPBS to state and local
government budgets).

ATLANTA ECONOMIC REVIEW
Welch, Oliver.
"The marriage of planning and budgeting in Georgia: a six-year
expenditure plan." Vol. 20, August 1970, p. 4-6. (Discusses
Georgia's plans for instituting a system to assure a comprehensive planning and programming process in their state
government).

BUDGETING
Botner, Stanley B.
"The states and PPBS." July/August 1968, p. 17-21. (Briefly
surveys some of the states implementing PPBS).

BUSINESS AND GOVERNMENT REVIEW
(University of Missouri)
Botner, Stanley B.
"Municipal budgeting: problems and developments."
March/April 1969. p. 14-26. (Discusses various U. S. cities).

JOURNAL OF SYSTEMS MANAGEMENT
Byron, R. J.
"Reviewing a program budget system in a municipality."
Vol. 22, April 1971, p. 33-39.

MANAGEMENT CONTROLS
Harrill, E. Reece.
"A financial management system for local governments."
Vol. 17, Feb. 1970, p. 27-34. (Outlines and illustrates elements
of a system).

MANAGERIAL PLANNING
Denhardt, Robert B. and David F. Paulsen.
"PPBS and the cities." May/June 1969, p. 13-17.

MIDWEST REVIEW OF PUBLIC ADMINISTRATION
Behan, R. W.
"The PPBS controversy: a conflict of ideologies."
Vol. 4, No. 1, Feb. 1970, p. 3-16.
Markham, Emerson and William C. McConkey.
"PPBS as aid to decision making." Vol. 3, Feb. 1969, p. 65-71.

MUNICIPAL FINANCE
Blick, Larry N.
"A new look at capital improvements programming."
Vol. 42, No. 2, Nov. 1969, p. 110-116.

Cotton, John F.
"Planning-programming-budgeting systems for local
government." Vol. 41, August 1968, p. 26-33.

Donaho, John A.
"Planning-programming-budgeting systems."
Vol. 40, No. 1, August 1970, p. 17-25.

Hunt, Alfred L.
"Budgetary accounting — its role in fiscal control."
Vol. 41, No. 1, August 1968, p. 43-49.

Luther, Robert A.
"PPBS in Fairfax County: a practical experience."
Vol. 41, No. 1, August 1968, p. 34-42.

"PPBS and accounting."
Vol. 41, No. 3, February 1969, p. 122-131, 134-137. (Contents:
Accounting problems of planning-programming-budgeting sys-
tems, by Jay H. Gordon. — PPBS in Dayton, Ohio, by Nicholas
M. Meiszer. — PPBS and accounting in San Diego, by William
G. Sage and James J. Holodnak. — Integrated information
systems for large and small municipalities, by Gary A. Luing).

"PPBS and other budget applications."
Vol. 4, No. 4, May 1969, p. 148-176. (Contents: An approach to
implementing PPB, by Larry N. Blick. — Organizing for a new
approach to budgeting, by Monty C. Lish. — Assessing the
future, by Robert L. Johnson. — Budgeting for parks and recreation by Joseph L. Rochford. — Budgeting for the public

works dept., by James P. Wright, Jr. and Gerald S. Tyson. Application of PPBS to local government budgeting).

NATION'S CITIES
Hearle, Edward F. R.
"Designing urban information systems." April 1970, p. 16-19. (Discusses the use of social indicators to measure the quality of urban life).

POLICE CHIEF
Doland, John F.
"The P-P-B (planning, programming and budgeting) concept." July 1968, p. 28, 30,
Leahy, Frank J., Jr.
"Planning program budgeting system." July 1968, p. 16-27.
Pence, Gary.
"Program planning budgeting system (in the Dayton, Ohio Police Dept.)." Vol. 38, July 1971, p. 52-57.

PUBLIC ADMINISTRATION REVIEW
Alesch, D. J.
"Government in evolution: a real world focus for state planning." Vol. 28, No. 3, May/June 1968, p. 264-267. (Highlights PPBS in New York).

PUBLIC MANAGEMENT
Snyder, Ralph W.
"Reappraising program budgeting." May 1960, p. 99-101. (Deals with municipal budgeting policy).

QUARTERLY REVIEW OF ECONOMICS AND BUSINESS
Jones, Roger H.
"Program budgeting: fiscal facts and federal fancy." Vol. 9, Summer 1969, p. 45-57. (Discusses history, applications, benefits and problems at the state and local levels).

RHODE ISLAND BUSINESS QUARTERLY
Coletta, Edmund R.
"Analytic program budgeting in Rhode Island." Vol. 7, March 1971, p. 10-12.

STATE GOVERNMENT
Lauber, John C.
"PPBS in state government — Maryland's approach." Vol. 42, No. 1, Winter 1969, p. 31-37. (Explains Maryland's decision to adopt a Management Information and Evaluation System rather than a full PPB program).
Reynolds, John W.
"Program budgeting in Wisconsin." Vol. 37, No. 4, Autumn 1964, p. 210-215. (Describes implementation and predicts success).

WESTERN POLITICAL QUARTERLY
Shipman, George A.
"The program budget in state government." Vol. 14, No. 3, September 1961 supp., p. 71-72. (Notes the distinct shift from "administrative" type budgets to program or peformance budgets).

APPLICATIONS TO HIGHER EDUCATION

Monographs

Alioto, Robert F. and J. A. Jungherr.
Operational PPBS for education: a practical approach to effective decision making. New York, Harper, 1971. 325 p.

Association of School Business Officials.
Program planning-budgeting-evaluation system design: annotated bibliography. Chicago, Research Corp. of ASBO, 1968. 15 p.

Association of School Business Officials.
Report of the First National Conference on PPBS in Education, edited by Charles W. Foster. Chicago, Research Corporation of ASBO, 1969.

Banghart, Frank W.
Educational systems analysis. New York, Macmillan, 1969.

Benson, Charles.
The economics of public education, 2nd ed.
Boston, Houghton Mifflin, 1968.

Burkhead, Jesse, Thomas G. Fox and John W. Holland.
Input and output in large-city high schools.
New York, Syracuse University Press, 1967.

Bushnell, Don P. and Dwight W. Allen, eds.
The computer in American education. New York, Wiley, 1967.

Carpenter, M. B.
Analysis of educational programs. Santa Monica,
Rand Corp., 1971. 17 p.

Committee for Economic Development.
Research and Policy Committee.
Innovation in education: new directions for the American school. New York, CED, 1968.

Dobbins, Charles G. and Calvin B. T. Lee, eds.
Whose goals for American higher education?
Washington, D. C., American Council on Education, 1968.

Farquhar, J. A.
Accountability, program budgeting and the California educational information system: a discussion and a proposal.
Santa Monica, Rand Corp., 1971. 28 p.

Fitzsimmons, Warren Biggs.
A model for a public school program budget.
Ann Arbor, Michigan, University Microfilms, 1967. 110 p.

George Washington University. State-Local Finances Project.
Planning for educational development in a planning, programming, budgeting system, by Selma J. Mushkin.
Washington, D.C., Committee on Educational Finance, NEA, 1968.

Gross, Edward and Paul V. Grambsch.
University goals and academic power. Washington, D. C.,
American Council on Education, 1968.

Haggart, S. A., et al.
Program budgeting for school planning: concepts and applica-

tions. Englewood Cliffs, N. J., Educational Technology Publications, 1971.

Haggart, S. A.
The program structuring aspect of PPB for education.
Santa Monica, Rand Corp., 1971. 13 p.

Hansen, W. Lee and Burton W. Weisbrod.
Benefits, costs, and finance of public higher education.
Chicago, Markham, 1969.

Harris, Seymour E. and Alan Levenson, eds.
Education and public policy. Berkeley, McCuthchan, 1965.

Hartley, Harry J.
Educational planning-programming-budgeting.
Englewood Cliffs, N. J., Prentice-Hall, 1968. 290 p.

Hawaii. Department of Education.
An introduction to the planning-programming-budgeting system.
Honolulu, 1968.

Hill, LaMar Lucius.
Program budgeting in public school districts.
Ann Arbor, Michigan, University Microfilms, 1967.

Hirsch, W. Z.
Education in the program budget. Santa Monica, Rand Corp.
1965. 37 p.

Kershaw, J. A.
Systems analysis and education. Santa Monica, Rand Corp.,
1959. 64 p.

Levin, Melvin R. and Joseph S. Slavet.
Continuing education. Lexington, Mass., Heath, 1970. 139 p.

Levine, Donald M.
Some problems in planning-programming-budgeting for education. Cambridge, Mass., Harvard University Press, 1969.

Levine, Donald M.
Structuring program analysis for educational research.
Santa Monica, Rand Corp., 1971. 19 p.

Mansergh, Gerald G., ed.
Curricular and fiscal planning with planning, programming,
budgeting systems. Detroit, Metropolitan Detroit Bureau
of School Studies, 1969. 42 p.

Miller, James L.
State budgeting for higher education: the use of formulas and
cost analysis. Ann Arbor, Michigan, Inst. of Public
Administration, U. of Michigan, 1964.

National School Public Relations Association.
PPBS and the school: new system promotes efficiency,
accountability. Washington, D. C., NSPRA, 1972.

Organization for Economic Co-operation and Development.
Budgeting, programme analysis and cost-effectiveness in
educational planning. Paris, Washington, D. C., OECD, 1968.

Organization for Economic Co-operation and Development.
Mathematic models in educational planning.
Paris, Washington, D. C., OECD, 1967.

Psacharopoulos, George.
The rate of return on investment in education at the regional level. Honolulu, Economic Research Center, University of Hawaii, 1969.

Stromsdorfer, Ernst W.
Economic concepts and criteria for vocational education. Toronto, OISE, 1967. 30 p.

Swanson, John E., Wesley Arden and Homer E. Still, Jr.
Financial analysis of current operations of colleges and universities. Ann Arbor, Michigan, Institute of Public Administration, University of Michigan, 1966.

Terrey, John N.
Program budgeting and other newer management tools in higher education: a description and annotated bibliography. Seattle, University of Washington, Center for the Development of Community College Education, 1968. 57 p.

Texas. University.
A planning, programming and budgeting (PPBS) approach to the University of Texas system, introductory pages to a preliminary report prepared by Albert Shapero. Austin, University of Texas, 1967.

Williams, Harry.
Planning for effective resource allocation in universities. Washington, D. C., American Council on Education, 1966.

APPLICATIONS TO HIGHER EDUCATION

Periodical Articles

ACADEMY OF MANAGEMENT JOURNAL
Dyer, J. S.
"Use of PPBS in a public system of higher education: is it cost effective?" Vol. 13, September 1970, p. 285-99. (Concludes that the benefits may outweigh the substantial cost of introducing and implementing PPBS in higher education).
Hamelman, P. W.
"Missions, matrices and university management." Vol. 13, March 1970, p. 35-47. (Advocates applying PPBS to higher education, but warns that doing so will not be simple).

AMERICAN ECONOMIC REVIEW
Bowen, William G. and T. Aldrich Finegan.
"Educational attainment and labor force participation." Vol. 56, May, 1966, p. 567-682.
"Economics of education."
Vol. 56, May 1966, p. 358-400. (Contents: Education and the distribution of earnings, by Garry S. Becker and Barry R. Criswick. — Investment in the education of the poor: a pessimistic report, by Eugene Smolensky. — Measurement of the quality of schooling, by Finis Welch).

AMERICAN EDUCATION
Lessinger, Leon.
"Accountability for results: a bsaic challenge for America's schools." Vol. 5, June-July 1969, p. 2-4.

AMERICAN SCHOOL BOARD JOURNAL
Baynham, D.
"PPBS and several good reasons it shouldn't scare you off." Vol. 158, August 1970, p. 27-29.
Exton, Elaine.
"State legislators urged to install planning-programming-budgeting system." Vol. 154, February 1967, p. 13-16. (Describes efforts of the National Committee for Support of the Public Schools to influence state and local officials to establish PPBS for education).
Szuberia, Charles A.
"How to ease into PPBS." Vol. 156, May 1969, p. 20. (Presents a sample analysis of expenditures — that of Niles Township Community High School District in the Chicago suburb of Skokie).
Wilsey, Carl E.
"Program Budgeting: an easy guide with the confusion removed; don't throw up your hands became PPBS has seemed so complicated — not, at least, until you've read this."
Vol. 156, May 1969, p. 16-20. (School district budgeting).

AMERICAN TEACHER
Bhaerman, Robert.
"In quest: the danger of program budgeting." Vol. 55,
October 1970.
Myers, Miles.
"The unholy marriage — accountants and curriculum makers."
Vol. 55, November 1970.

AMERICAN VOCATIONAL JOURNAL
Malinski, J. F.
"Minnesota implements the regional concept in a state committed
to PPBS." Vol. 44, November 1969, p. 36-8. (Explains some of
the concepts and techniques used by Minnesota in their com-
prehensive planning for vocational education).
Ristau, R. A.
"PPBS in business education." Vol. 46, March 1971, p. 45-8.

AUDIOVISUAL INSTRUCTION
Horton, R. L. and K. W. Bishop.
"Keeping up with the budget crunch." Vol. 15,
December 1970, p. 49-50.

BUSINESS AND ECONOMIC DIMENSIONS
Shagory, George E.
"Is the university ready for PPBS?" Vol. 7, Jan. 1971, p. 7-12.

BUSINESS EDUCATION FORUM
Ristau, R. A.
"Behavioral objectives in business education lead to PPBS."
Vol. 25, March 1971, p. 3-6.

BUSINESS WEEK
"How colleges cope with the red ink." November 21, 1970, p. 56-63.

CTA JOURNAL (California Teachers' Association)
Gordon, Garford G.
"The challenge of PPBS." Vol. 66, January 1970, p. 30-31.
(Reviews briefly the potential usefulness of PPBS in education).

COLLEGE AND UNIVERSITY BUSINESS
"Educators brush up on fiscal management." Vol. 47, Oct. 1969,
p. 71-5. (Describes one-week seminars for college administrators).
Severance, M. F.
"Accounting for decisions as well as dollars." Vol. 51,
November 1971, p. 58-60.
Sutterfield, W. D.
"College planning could use HELP." Vol. 50, March 1971. p. 42-6.
Wheatley, E.
"Putting management techniques to work for education."
Vol. 48, April 1970, p. 55-59. (Recommends adopting management
techniques when feasible).

COLLEGE MANAGEMENT
Brady, Ronald W.
"Budget system: key to planning." Vol. 5, January 1970, p. 45-7.
(Discusses system as applied at Ohio State University).

ECONOMIST
"PPB; what's school for?" Vol. 235, April 25, 1970, p. 20.
(Describes attempts to apply PPB to the British education
department).

EDUCATION
Wooton, L. M.
"Systems approach to education as viewed from the classroom."
Vol. 91, February 1971, p. 215-19.

EDUCATIONAL LEADERSHIP
Jones, D. M.
"PPBS: a tool for improving instruction." Vol. 28,
January 1971, p. 405-9.

EDUCATIONAL RECORD
Dilley, Frank B.
"Program budgeting in the university setting."
Vol. 47, Fall 1966, p. 474-489.
Eberle, August W. and Stephen C. McCutcheon.
"A system model for institutional planning."
Vol. 51, Winter 1970, p. 66-71.
Hollister, Robinson G., Jr.
"A decision-making budget for application to educational
institutions and research and developmental organizations."
Vol. 47, Fall 1966, p. 490-97.
Morrell, L. R.
"A look at program budgeting." Vol. 50, Summer 1969, p. 286-89.
(Reviews implementation of PPBS in colleges and universities).

EDUCATIONAL TECHNOLOGY
McGiveney, Joseph H.
"New systems' approaches to resource allocation decisions:
a second look." Vol. 9, December 1969, p. 31-4.
(Reviews developments and expresses guarded optimism).
Montello, P. A.
"PDM: a system for educational management; precedence
diagramming method." Vol. 11, December 1971, p. 62-4.
Mowbray, G. and J. B. Levine.
"Development and implementation of CAMPUS: a computer-
based planning and budgeting system for universities and
colleges." Vol. 11, May 1971, p. 27-32.
Sisson, R. L.
"Introduction to the educational-planning-programming-
budgeting system." Vol. 12, February 1972, p. 54-60.
Tanner, C. K.
"Educational operations research: an approach to PPBS
implementation." Vol. 11, December 1971, p. 50-1.

EDUCATIONAL THEORY
LaBrecque, R.
"Social planning and the imperium humanum: John Dewey circa

1960's." Vol. 19, Fall 1969, p. 363-71. (Appraises PPBS as planning tool in education).

HIGH SCHOOL JOURNAL

Poindexter, Charles C.
"Planning-programming-budgeting systems for education."
Vol. 52, January 1969, p. 206-17. (Explains promise and problems of PPBS for education).

INTERNATIONAL SOCIAL SCIENCE JOURNAL

"Economics of education."
Vol. 14, no. 4, 1962, p. 619-718. (Contents: Introduction, by John Vaizey. — The economics of education in the USSR, by Stanislav Strumilin. — Social returns to education, by Mary Jean Bowman. — The concept of human capital, by M. Debeauvais. — Teaching methods and their costs, by Charles Benson. — Education and economic development, by Arthur Lewis. — Administration and the economics of education, by Howard Hayden. — Economic and social aspects of the planning of education, by H. M. Phillips).

JOURNAL OF ACCOUNTANCY

Rappaport, Donald
"New approaches in public education (PPB; decentralization)."
Vol. 126, July 1968, p. 31-42. (Describes three approaches: PPB, decentralized decision centers, and educational information centers).

JOURNAL OF HIGHER EDUCATION

Peterson, M. W.
"Potential impact of PPBS on colleges and universities."
Vol. 42, January 1971, p. 1-20.

Thompson, D. L.
"PPBS: the need for experience." Vol. 42, Nov. 1971, p. 678-91.

JOURNAL OF RESEARCH AND DEVELOPMENT
IN EDUCATION

Fogel, R. L.
"Conditions for the use of PPB." Vol. 3, Summer 1970, p. 72-9.

JOURNAL OF SECONDARY EDUCATION

Carter, V.
"PPBS in a smal high school: it can be done."
Vol. 45, November 1970, p. 313-19.

Livingston, J. A.
"Educational goals and program planning budgeting system (PPBS)." Vol. 45, November 1970, p. 305-12.

LIBERAL EDUCATION

Parden, R. J.
"Planning, programming and budgeting systems."
Vol. 57, May 1971, p. 202-10.

Weathersby, G. B.
"PPBS; purpose, persuasion, backbone and spunk."
Vol. 57, May 1971, p. 211-18.

MANAGEMENT CONTROLS
Berg, Richard D.
   "A PPBS overview — for the school district."
   Vol. 19, January 1972, p. 13-17.
Perkins, Joseph A.
   "PPBS for education." Vol. 17, February 1970, p. 23-26.
   (Advocates use of PPBS in education).

NEA RESEARCH BULLETIN
Dorsey, John W.
   "Planning-programming-budgeting (PPB)."
   Vol. 47, October 1969, p. 94-95.
"What is a programming, planning, budgeting system?"
   Vol. 46, December 1968, p. 112-13.

NATIONAL TAX JOURNAL
"Some benefit-cost considerations of universal junior college
   education." Vol. 19, March 1966, p. 48-57.

NATION'S SCHOOLS
Curtis, William H.
   "Program budgeting design for schools unveiled, with much
   work still to go." Vol. 84, November 1969, p. 40-43. (Interview
   with the design developer of a three-year project: PPBS).
Gibbs, Wesley F., et al.
   "PPBS: what we've learned in one year." Vol. 84, November 1969,
   p. 43. (Describes experience of District 68, Skokie, Illinois).
Gibbs, Wesley F.
   "Program budgeting filters down to education."
   Vol. 82, November 1968, p. 51-3.
Grieder Calvin.
   "PPBS and assessment: where trouble could erupt."
   Vol. 83, June 1969, p. 8. (Warns that PPBS may place undue
   emphasis on measurable aspects of elementary and secondary
   schooling).
Grieder, Calvin.
   "Program budgeting may not solve your planning problems."
   Vol. 81, June 1968, p. 8. (Cities five serious shortcomings of
   the new system).
Kent, Arthur E.
   "How Skokie created a program budget."
   Vol. 82, November 1968, p. 56-59.
Rath, Gustave J.
   "PPBS is more than a budget: it's a total planning process."
   Vol. 82, November 1968, p. 53-55.

NORTH CENTRAL ASSOCIATION QUARTERLY
Chambers, George A.
   "PPBS: new challenges and opportunities for the principal in
   financial planning and management."
   Vol. 42, Spring 1968, p. 301-6.

OPERATIONAL RESEARCH QUARTERLY
Hitch, Charles J.
"Systems approach to decision-making in the Department of Defense and the University of California." Vol. 19, April 1968, p. 37-45. (Special conference issue).

PHI DELTA KAPPAN
Alioto, Robert F. and J. A. Jungherr.
"Using PPBS to overcome taxpayers' resistance."
Vol. 51, November 1969, p. 138-141.
Cyphert, Frederick R., and Walter L. Gant.
"The Delphi technique: a case study." Vol. 52, January 1971.
Durstine, Richard M.
"An accountability information system." Vol. 52, December 1970.
Furno, Orlando F.
"Planning, programming, budgeting systems: boon or bane?" Vol. 51, November 1969, p. 142-4.

POPULAR GOVERNMENT
Williams, Robert T.
"Speak to me — in PPB: now we can show returns on dollars spent for education." Vol. 35, April 1969, p. 5-9. (Discusses techniques used in North Carolina community colleges to measure educational programs in terms of quantitative output).

SCHOOL MANAGEMENT
Buskin, Martin.
"PPBS means better money management." Vol. 13, November 1969, p. 64-8. (Discusses experience of school districts in New Hyde Park and Pearl River, New York; Westport and Darien, Connecticut; and Milford, New Hampshire).
Lehman, G. O.
"Nine pitfalls of PPBS." Vol. 16, January 1972, p. 2.
Scott, D. H.
"How PPBS is being used in California." Vol. 15, Feb. 1971 p. 12-15.
Tanzman, J.
"Planning your media program's future." Vol. 14, July 1970, p. 40.

SOUTHERN ECONOMIC JOURNAL
Stubblebine, William C.
"Institutional elements in the financing of education."
Vol. 22, July 1965, p. 15-38.
Wiseman, Jack.
"Cost-benefit analysis in education." Vol. 32, July 1965, p. 1-14.

TAX DIGEST
Hitch, Charles J.
"Program budgeting in a university setting." 2nd quarter, 1968, p. 13-19. (Describes PPB as a system "...designed to inject needed efficiency into the decision-making process in any organization, private or public." The author is an originator and continued proponent of PPBS).

APPLICATIONS TO LIBRARIES

Monographs

Dougherty, R. M. and Fred J. Heinritz.
Scientific management of library operations. New York,
Scarecrow, 1966, 258 p.

Milliman, Jerome W. and Richard L. Pfister.
Economic aspects of library service in Indiana. Indiana Library
Studies, Report No. 7, Indiana State Library, 1970. 147 p.

Morey, G. E.
Identification of common library goals, objectives and activities
relative to a planning, programming, budgeting system. Thesis,
Western Michigan University, 1970.

Morse, Philip M.
Library effectiveness: a system approach. Cambridge,
MIT Press, 1968. 207 p.

Raffel, Jeffrey A. and Robert Shishko.
Systematic analysis of university libraries: an application of
cost-benefit analysis to the M.I.T. libraries. Cambridge,
MIT, 1969. 107 p.

U. S. Department of Health, Education, and Welfare, Education
Office.
Statewide long-range planning for libraries, report of conference.
September 19-22, 1965, Chicago Illinois, sponsored by Library
Services Branch; edited by Herbert A. Carl, Washington, D. C.,
1966. 59 p.

APPLICATIONS TO LIBRARIES

Periodical Articles

ALA BULLETIN
Young, Helen
"Performance and program budgeting: an annotated bibliography." Vol. 61, No. 1, January 1967, p. 63-67.

AMERICAN LIBRARIES
Summers, William.
"A change in budgetary thinking." Vol. 2, December 1971,
p. 1174-1180. (Reviews major budgetary systems and their
applicability to libraries with some emphasis on
performance budgeting).

Howard, Edward N.
"Toward PPBS in the public library." Vol. 2, April 1971,
p. 386-393. (Describes use of PPBS by a medium-size public
library — that of Vigo County).

CALIFORNIA SCHOOL LIBRARIES
Holland, E. D.
"Initials PPBS stand for planning, programming, budgeting
system." Vol. 41, May 1970, p. 143-144.

COLLEGE AND RESEARCH LIBRARIES
Axford, William
"An approach to performance budgeting at the Florida Atlantic
University Library." Vol. 32, March 1971, p. 87-104. (Summarizes
problems encountered at FAU in 1967. Supplies the Clapp-Jordan
and University of Washington formulae for budgeting).
Keller, John E.
"Program budgeting and cost-benefit analysis in libraries." Vol.
30, March 1969, p. 156-160. (Points out likelihood that these
systems will be applied to most libraries in the near future).

LAW LIBRARY JOURNAL
Schultz, John S.
"Program budgeting and work measurement for law libraries."
Vol. 63, August 1970, p. 353-362. (Offers concrete suggestions
for implementing a new budget system).

LIBRARY JOURNAL
Hamill, Harold L.
"Numbers game." Vol. 90, Sept. 15, 1965, p. 3563-3566. (Warns
of the problems involved when attempting to interpret the
library's operation in terms of numerical measurement and
units of output).
Jenkins, Harold R.
"The ABC's of PPB: an explanation of how planning-program-
ming-budgeting can be used to improve the management of
libraries." Vol. 96, Oct. 1, 1971, p. 3089-3093.
Meyers, J. K. and R. Barber.
"McNamara, media and you." Vol. 96, March 15,1971, p. 1079-1081.
(Explains how to apply PPBS to school media programs).
Price, Paxton P.
"Performance budgeting in practice." Vol. 84, March 15, 1959,
p. 797+. (Evaluates the methods, advantages, and limitations
of a library program (performance) budget).

LIBRARY TRENDS
Price, Paxton P.
"Budgeting and budget controls in public libraries." Vol. 11,
April 1963, p. 402-414. (Reviews the development
of a performance budget).

LIBRARY WORLD (London)
Colley, D. I.
"Planning, programming, budgeting system (PPBS)." Vol. 72,
Feb. 1971, p. 237-238. (Reviews, in a down-to-earth manner, the
application of PPBS to libraries).

OKLAHOMA LIBRARIAN
Green, J.
"Automated responsibility reporting for libraries; a program
budgeting and reporting system recently installed in the Oklahoma department of libraries." Vol. 20. January 1970, p. 18-21.

PENNSYLVANIA LIBRARY ASSOCIATION BULLETIN
Baldwin, Daniel R.
"Managerial competence and librarians." Vol. 26, January 1971, p. 17-25. (Advises library management to examine new techniques, including PPBS, used by management in other fields).

SCHOOL LIBRARIES
Lambo, Diana L.
"Approaches to accountability." Vol. 21, Fall 1971, p. 15-19. (Reacts to President Nixon's educational reform speech).
Wedgeworth, R.
"Budgeting for school media centers." Vol. 20, Spring 1971, p. 29-36. (Explores some of the problems involved in budgeting for school libraries and/or media centers).

SPECIAL LIBRARIES
Fazar, Willard.
"Program planning and budgeting theory; improved library effectiveness by use of the planning-programming-budgeting system." Vol. 60, Sept. 1969, p. 423-433. (Discusses Dept. of Defense use of PPB and its spread into nongovernmental units).
